Brimming with creative inspiration, how-to projects and useful information to enrich your everyday life, Quarto Knows is a favourite destination for those pursuing their interests and passions. Visit our site and dig deeper with our books into your area of interest: Quarto Creates, Quarto Cooks, Quarto Homes, Quarto Lives, Quarto Drives, Quarto Explores, Quarto Gifts, or Quarto Kids.

First published in 2018 by White Lion Publishing, an imprint of The Quarto Group.
The Old Brewery, 6 Blundell Street
London, N7 9BH,
United Kingdom
T (0)20 7700 6700
www.QuartoKnows.com

A catalogue record for this book is available from the British Library.

ISBN 978 1 78131 802 7
Ebook ISBN 978 1 78603 871 5

10 9 8 7 6 5 4 3 2

Design by Paileen Currie
Illustrations by Yelena Bryksenkova

Printed in China

THE HAPPINESS PASSPORT

A world tour of
joyful living in
50 words

MEGAN C HAYES PhD

ILLUSTRATED BY
YELENA BRYKSENKOVA

Contents

CHAPTER FOUR

Joy & Spirituality

CHAPTER FIVE

Balance & Calm

Happiness
Around the World

Our world is made up of many thousands of languages and dialects, spoken in almost two hundred countries by countless communities made up of billions of individuals. As this global population becomes increasingly interconnected, we grow ever more fascinated by the 'untranslatable' nature of words that hide in the cultural corners of our planet. Each expresses – with poignancy and precision – an intriguing idea unique to the place it calls home.

An idea that seems to be of perennial interest to us all, however – and that has reigned in nearly every society since the ancients – is how humans can live *well*. This desire unites us like nothing else, while at once provoking countless interpretations across our world's many tongues. Is the good life characterised by sharing food and conversation with loved ones, epitomised in the Spanish term *sobremesa* and the notion of *liming* from Trinidad and Tobago? Or is living well perhaps better described as having the grit and determination to overcome difficult times, typified by the Finnish concept of *sisu*?

In joining the dots between these differing shades of the satisfying life, might we find the secrets of truly living well? Could we cultivate an ever-richer vocabulary of happiness – and one that we can all speak? This book aspires to do exactly that.

Are words ever truly 'untranslatable'?

The 'untranslatable' nature of these words is actually something of a misnomer. Such words fascinate us precisely because they *do* translate to an emotional, social or physical experience that we can each understand. We just may not have found a word for it until now. Our instant recognition of these concepts – from the strikingly simple to the wonderfully weird – accentuates our similarities, even as it helps us revere our respective cultural quirks.

From the Danish *hygge* to the Australian Aboriginal term *dadirri*, and from the Catalan *seny* to the Japanese *ikigai* – in these pages you will find both familiar and surprising terms, each illuminating a different hue of happiness. Each word connects us across cultures, revealing both disarming disparity *and* a truly collective quest for the life well lived.

How these words were chosen

Clearly, this book is not exhaustive – there are many words that were not included and many more still that remain tucked away within their own cultures, undiscovered by the wider world like buried treasure. The selection was made to give as broad and varied a picture as possible, both of our many diverse cultures and of the different kinds of happiness we can experience.

Some words are light-hearted, like the English *whimsy* or the French *bon vivant* – and some showcase a far deeper side to our happiness, like the Sanskrit *ātman* or the Haudenosaunee *uki-okton*. All were chosen because they portray something surprising yet recognisable: each word distinguishes us and unites us. Each word enriches our view of happiness, yet somehow affirms a feeling we have known all along.

The bittersweet side of happiness

Happiness is not a static state, and in fact involves a much more intricate medley of emotions than we usually give it credit for – why else would we cry 'tears of joy', for example, or have the sensation of missing someone even before they leave? As such, there were many 'bitter-sweet' words that did not make it into the main pages of this book. While these may not be the chirpiest of terms, they do illustrate the complex and interwoven nature of our happier and unhappier emotions. For example, what is particularly striking is how many words and expressions we have around the world for yearning and longing – illustrating how we pine for that which makes us truly happy. These include the Welsh *hiraeth* – a nostalgic ache for an ideal home, perhaps one we have never really known – and the very similar *saudade* in Portuguese, loosely meaning the desire for something that does not exist. There is the Romanian *dor*, a word with many meanings for different individuals, but that is characterised by a deep and profound longing – for loved ones, places or something forever lost. The Trinidadian Creole *tabanca* describes a feeling of lingering heartbreak or pining (particularly for carnival season!), while the Irish Gaelic *cumha* evokes a similarly melancholic desire, or homesickness.

These words of yearning serve as a reminder to notice happiness *as it happens*, in the form of the people, places and experiences we love. This is, hopefully, exactly what the words in this book will inspire you to do.

A NOTE FROM THE AUTHOR

In joyfully compiling this compendium of words, I have done my utmost to accurately and respectfully represent those chosen. However, given that these many languages and cultures are not my own, I anticipate that I may not have achieved this flawlessly in every case. I hope that the generous reader will forgive me any inadvertent errors, and will enjoy the book as it has been intended: a celebration of the many manifestations of happiness to be found around our globe.

I would like to give a special mention to Dr Tim Lomas who, with great insight and sensitivity, has pioneered research in this area with "The Happy Words Project". Those interested in this wealth of research aimed at understanding wellbeing from a cross-cultural perspective will find his book, *The Happiness Dictionary: Words from Around the World to Help Us Lead a Richer Life* (Piatkus, 2018), an inspiring read.

Chapter One

Home & Environment

Picture a cosy room with a crackling fire, the lull of familiar voices in easy conversation, and perhaps a table laden with dishes of delicious food that can be tasted nowhere else but here ... The word *home* holds these and many other connotations. Home is – proverbially speaking – where the heart is, and apparently there's no place like it. It stirs our most deeply felt emotions.

Thoughts of home bring to mind intimate, safe and familiar places – but around the world our diverse languages illuminate how our sense of home can also extend far beyond this. We find comfort in our Earth's many environs – including those that are wild and remote. The crunch of leaves under foot in autumnal woodland can make us feel the sense of peace we associate with being 'at home'. At other times we feel most at home in the freedom and scope of open spaces. And, of course, sometimes home is not a physical place at all – not somewhere we can point out on a map – but a place that exists between people.

Let's see how our differing environments – and the many unique ways in which we speak about them – affect how we feel, and how we find happiness.

GÖKOTTA

jɜ:ku:tə | noun | Swedish

1. to rise at dawn in order to go outside and hear the first birdsong

Swedish is a language rich in descriptions of how we can draw a sense of belonging and happiness from the natural world. One word that perhaps best illustrates this is *gökotta*. A *gökotta* is literally a 'dawn picnic' sound-tracked by early birdsong, but can also refer more generally to an appreciation of nature. While for most of us our mornings are defined less by tranquil experiences like these and more by beeping alarm clocks, strong coffee and eating a hurried breakfast before we rush out the door to work, *gökotta* is a gentle reminder that things do not always have to be this way. Sometimes, it is okay to schedule a little more of this life's less practical tasks into our busy routines.

Gökotta is unlikely to be something we schedule in every morning, but occasionally slipping out of bed at daybreak and strolling outside for an early burst

of the natural world may just do wonders for our sense of well-being. This is because it encompasses many feel-good factors: rising early, mindfulness, exercise (if our *gökotta* includes a walk) and time in nature. Start your morning the *gökotta* way and try not to have a spring in your step for the rest of the day.

Yet this is not the only word the Swedes possess for positive experiences in nature. If the Swedish people start their day with *gökotta*, then when dusk comes it is time to revere *mångata* – describing the road-like reflection that the moon makes across water at night. *Mångata* evokes the contemplative mood that such ephemeral natural wonders can stir within us – and shows how the Swedes derive joy from nature at all times of day.

Another particularly beautiful word in the Swedish language that similarly articulates the happiness we so often source from our environment is *smultronställe*. This literally means 'place of wild strawberries' but can refer more generally to any tucked away and highly treasured place. *Mitt smultronställe* therefore means 'my hideaway' or 'my special place', and can evoke any environment where we feel happy, content, peaceful and truly at home. There we have it: if there is one group of people whose well-being is intricately intertwined with their environment, it's the Swedes.

'ĀINA

a:i:na: | noun | Hawaiian

1. land (or 'that which feeds us')

There is one environment so fundamental to our survival on this planet that we rarely stop to ponder the happiness it brings: land, the official home of all human beings. Were it not for this bountiful, muddy mass underfoot ... well, let's just say that even the best swimmers among us would be pretty scuppered. Accordingly, one place where people take their land very seriously is among the islands of Hawaii. In Hawaiian language – an Austronesian language spoken by around eight thousand people – the word for land, 'āina, has the deeper meaning of 'that which feeds us'. How often do you think this way about the ground you walk upon? My guess would be rarely, if ever. For Hawaiians however, the beautiful phrase aloha 'āina – literally 'love of the land' – captures the significance of 'āina to Hawaiian culture and identity.

Aloha 'āina represents a way of living with love and reverence for both land and sea (two pretty important elements in island life) stretching from ancient mythology all the way to current environmental debates. This passion for 'āina manifests within Hawaiian culture through everything from storytelling, chanting and traditional celebratory hula dancing, to more practical things like agriculture and politics. On an individual level, our sense of aloha 'āina might be expressed through lifestyle practices founded upon deep respect for our environment. In this sense, then, anything from prayer to everyday recycling might be considered one expression of our aloha 'āina.

The reverent feelings the Hawaiian people have for their 'āina highlights the importance of showing gratitude for one of our most precious natural resources. Very few, in fact, could be called more precious. This could potentially have many benefits, not least in how we treat our planet, but also because intentional gratitude has shown to be one of the principal ways in which we can impact our individual well-being. By noting and saying thank you for the many things we often take for granted, we are able to remind ourselves just how lucky we are. Let the word 'āina serve us as a reminder – and a very important one – to appreciate this lush and abundant planet we call home.

The great outdoors

A love story

If you are seeking a fail-safe lift of the spirits then you need look no further than outside your own front door – literally. Connection with nature has been shown to positively impact our psychological well-being, sense of meaning in life and our vitality. This makes sense, really, given that humans have only lived indoors for a fractional portion of their existence upon this Earth and yet we now spend an increasing amount of our lives hemmed in by concrete. Across cultures and languages we find lots of idiosyncratic ways to talk about this affinity we share for being outside. In English, there are several rare words that romantically depict nature, such as *psithurism* (the sound of wind whispering through the trees) or *petrichor* (a noun that describes the pleasantly earthy smell of the rain after a long period of dry, warm weather). The Dutch people have the verb *uitwaaien* – meaning to take a refreshing walk in the wind. In Canada, the charming term *sugar-weather* describes the warm days and cool nights of early spring – perfect conditions for maple trees to produce their sweet sap. Meanwhile, the Japanese have a word for the delicate beauty of sunlight dappled through treetops: *komorebi* (木漏れ日). Finally, the Irish Gaelic word *aoibhneas* captures the blissful feeling of having our senses filled by stunning scenery and fine weather – proving that perhaps our greatest romance is, indeed, the great outdoors.

HYGGE

hy:gə | noun | Danish and Norwegian
1. the practice of creating cosy and congenial environments
    that promote emotional well-being

Not simply a word but a whole system for happier living, *hygge* is a term found in both Denmark and Norway (originating in the Norwegian word for 'well-being') that has become increasingly popular in recent years outside of its Scandinavian homelands. Many things can be *hygge*, but certain items and experiences are widely considered to be almost synonymous with the term: candlelit spaces, red wine, woolly socks, a few close friends, the sound of beating rain outside of the window while you snuggle on the sofa under layers of soft blankets ... namely, anything that evokes an atmosphere of homely, heart-warming congeniality.

There are several variants of this cosy concept to be found across Northern European languages – reflecting how the dark and cool climes of these countries have compelled their inhabitants to create their own warmth. Sometimes this is through carefully crafted cosy spaces, but is also often found in the close feelings between people.

Another word that similarly evokes environments that are cosy and convivial is the Dutch *gezelligheid*, which captures a certain heartfelt and inviting ambience that many say typifies Dutch culture. A delightful canal-side picnic with friends would be *gezellig*, for example, but it could also describe the feeling of seeing a good friend again after a long separation. While the word has parallels with the Danish *hygge*, one important and unique distinction is the stronger sense of sociability that *gezelligheid* evokes (it originates from the word *gezel* meaning 'companion'), subtly different to the often more closed-off cosiness of *hygge*.

The German word *gemütlichkeit* also shares similarities with *hygge*. This many-layered term describes the comfortable sense of well-being we feel when in environments of good cheer and good food (or drink) with good company – and particularly the warm sense of social acceptance that accompanies these situations.

The Swedish have *mysig* for the feeling of pleasant, comfortable cosiness. For the Norwegians, a comparable word is *koselig*, which can apply to environments that are pleasant, but also to people – friends or children – that are affable. What is special about all of these words is their intertwining of environments with our friends, relatives and loved ones – illustrating that it is not usually just places themselves that shelter or boost the spirit, but the people we find there.

PROSTOR (ПРОСТОР)

pre'stor | noun | Russian

1. open space, expanse, vastness, scope
2. freedom

At times, we humans feel happiest in cosy, contained spaces – and at other times quite the opposite. Perhaps because of our ancestral, nomadic nature, we often find a deep joy in expansive spaces, and in few other environments are humans faced with such expansive immensity as in Russia. Which brings us to the lyrical Russian word *prostor*, also found in other Slavic languages, which captures that ephemeral, soul-stirring sensation that sweeping horizons can awaken in us.

Prostor encapsulates a yearning for wide plains, and is a good example of how we often link external landscapes metaphorically with our internal ones. A word associated closely to *prostor* is *dusha* (душа), the Russian word for soul or spirit. The expansiveness of our spirit, or *dusha*, finds an external reflection of itself in *prostor*, and this moment of inner and

outer harmony can feel deeply moving. Such a correspondence between our interior realm and our environment is what makes *prostor* such a uniquely special word, but it also illustrates something we can witness all around the globe: the profound way in which humans can feel connected to their environment, whatever that environment may be.

Interestingly, because of the internal vastness of *dusha*, *prostor* can also be felt in small spaces if, for example, we are accompanied by a great book. In even the tiniest and most closed-in of spaces, a good story can expand our interior horizons and offer us a sense of inner freedom.

What gives you a sense of *prostor*? Whether it's the seeming infinitude of the Siberian desert or the verdant moors of northern England (or even just in the pages of a good novel), the world is filled with expansive spaces that humans have navigated, conquered and called home since time immemorial. Next time you find yourself feeling cramped by your office cubicle or restricted by your railway commute, consider how you could seek out more *prostor*. Whether it's a trip to the coast or just a stroll around your local park, it may just give your *dusha* a much-needed lift.

CWTCH

kʊtʃ | noun | Welsh

1. a cupboard or cubbyhole
2. a cuddle or hug

Few words better illustrate how environments are not always strictly physical places, but can be created between people, than the Welsh term *cwtch*. There is an expression that anyone can cuddle, but only the Welsh can *cwtch* – a little word used to evoke anything from snuggling and affection, to sheltering and claiming, to a cosy place, and in fact, referring to all of these in one. When we give someone a *cwtch*-type embrace, the most concise description may be that we are offering him or her 'a safe place' – evoking the alternative meaning of the word: a cubbyhole. Yet even this description fails to capture the strong element of intimacy and privacy that the word conjures – either in a physical space or metaphorically between people. While typically thought of as a noun, *cwtch* is also used in everyday Welsh conversation as a verb, similarly to the English 'cuddle'. One might say, 'go on, cwtch up to me', or that they have been 'cwtching'.

Perhaps only truly comprehended in all its nuances by Welsh speakers themselves, *cwtch* is a word that suggests safeguarding and ownership of those we love, and can apply in both romantic and more platonic relationships – between lovers, friends or relatives. Because the word is so deeply bound up with warm relationships between individuals, it therefore relates strongly to happiness and well-being. Who among us has not been pulled back from the brink by the warm and resolute embrace of someone who loves us deeply? Sometimes a cuddle is so much more than a cuddle – and, in these instances, we are the beneficiaries of a *cwtch*.

Cwtch can evoke memories of childhood, rousing that safe, held, supported feeling that only our closest caregiver could provide when, as children, we scraped our knee or felt disappointed by the world – whether this was a tender hug from our mum or dad, or another reassuring figure.

Next time you offer (or are offered) a cuddle, think about the sheltered and protected space that is brought to life by this most ordinary of gestures – a space where all of us can find sustenance, reassurance and happiness any time it is needed.

TŪRANGAWAEWAE

tu:ræŋəwaiwai | noun | Māori

1. a place where one has the right to stand; place where one has rights of residence and belonging through kinship and whakapapa (genealogy)

This heavy-duty word combines *tūranga* (standing place) with *waewae* (feet), and although it is sometimes simply translated as 'a place to stand', it evokes far more than this. Our *tūrangawaewae* is our foundation, the place to which we feel most tied and where we feel our roots are – whether in a geographical or cultural sense. Accordingly, our *tūrangawaewae* is usually the place where we feel most empowered – a robust source of happiness.

Like many other words from around the globe linking us to our external environment, *tūrangawaewae* illustrates how connected outer landscapes are with our innermost landscapes. For the Māori people – as is the case for most of us – the moving scenes, trickling streams, mighty peaks and winding pathways of our home soil can stir within us a deep sense of security and rootedness. These environments offer us the strength to face life head on. If you have ever had the warm feeling of returning home from a foreign holiday by airplane and glimpsing that first sight of your own country from the air – then you will have some idea of the vigour of being in your own *tūrangawaewae*.

A similar feeling is evoked by the Spanish noun *querencia*, which describes the strength and resolve to be found within ourselves when we feel at home. In the Spanish tradition of bullfighting, the bull's *querencia* is the place to which he returns in the ring in order to regain his strength and footing. In his *querencia*, the bull is at his most powerful and therefore his most formidable.

We are often encouraged to get out of our comfort zones and experience the new, and so tend to focus less on how our *tūrangawaewae* – our standing place – can deeply empower us. Whether we find this literally in returning to our home town for a visit, or in holding a meeting at work in our own office rather than that of a colleague – physical spaces where we feel at home can make us feel more in control and, as a result, deeply well. Keep your own *tūrangawaewae* in mind next time you need a personal power supercharge.

WALDEINSAMKEIT

'valt?aɪnzaːmkaɪt | noun | German

1. forest solitude (the feeling of being alone in the woods)

For those of us lucky enough to have spent our childhoods near deciduous forests, memories will likely be stored firmly in our hearts of sun-dappled tree-climbing, the scent of mossy fallen logs and elated jumping in piles of golden leaves. In fact, the poet Ralph Waldo Emerson once wrote that, in the forest, we are always children. This idea evokes the sense of innocence, curiosity and quiet reverence that only a stroll through the woods can offer, and which is captured by *waldeinsamkeit*.

A German compound word that combines the terms for 'forest' (*wald*) and 'solitude' (*einsamkeit)*, this isn't a term you'll usually find in everyday conversation among German speakers, but rather reflects a poetic romanticism about being in nature. The Romantic writer Ludwig Tieck first coined this word, illuminating the special significance of Germany's great swathes of forest to its people through time.

Although *waldeinsamkeit* evokes solitude or loneliness among the quiet shade of great trees, it tends to be considered a positive, life-

affirming brand of solitude. It is the sensation whereby we are quiet and undistracted enough to feel that deep connection we have with the natural world. Interestingly, the Japanese have a similar term for the practice of finding well-being among trees: *shinrin-yoku* (森林浴) or 'forest bathing'.

These words highlight how woodland – so often used symbolically in fairytales as a magical, transitional realm – reconnects us powerfully with our untamed inner natures. The woods are wild, as we once were – the very antithesis of our civilised towns and cities.

In modern life, few of us can say we spend much time connected to our 'wild side' in this way. So much of our busy lives are spent indoors, feeling fraught, over-committed and multi-tasking. No wonder we forget ourselves. In the special, majestic silence of the forest – which is not silence at all but filled with the curious chirping of birds and the evocative rustle of leaves in the breeze – we find a solitude that helps us to return to ourselves. This meditative and grounded state is readily facilitated by our experiences with our most ancient friends: trees, highlighting the exceptional importance of ensuring we all allow a little *waldeinsamkeit* into our lives whenever possible.

FRILUFTSLIV

fri:luf:tsli:v | noun | Norwegian and Swedish
1.   Camp; outdoor life

Human beings have long had a talent for crafting homes in even the harshest of environments. We have built adobe huts to shelter us against the baking sun, constructed igloos to shield us from sub-zero temperatures and raised elegant tipis to protect the flames of our fires against the rolling winds of the Great Plains. These kinds of homes have made it possible for us to live and thrive smack-dab in the heart of the world's wildest places. What is more is that these types of homes – unlike our modern-day apartment blocks – exemplify a certain harmony and affinity between the natural world and our human agenda. In this sense, the people who have lived in such places likely got a much greater daily dose of what the Norwegian and Swedish people call *friluftsliv* (literally 'free-air life').

If you have ever had the pleasure of peeking your head out of a tent and breathing in the cool dewy scent of a forest or mountain range, watching the morning sky gradually lose its pink hue as the heat of the sun intensifies ... then you'll likely have some sense of the meaning of *friluftsliv*. This is not merely a word but a philosophy. *Friluftsliv* articulates a lifestyle of untethered living in tune with the natural world, and captures the feeling of spiritual kinship we have with such wild places. It highlights how experiences of connectedness to nature can be both joyous and transformative. They may even offer us a quasi-religious sense of having gained greater consciousness and wholeness of being.

Friluftsliv is a particularly important aspect to the lives and happiness of Norwegian people, connecting them to their landscape of majestic fjords, mountain peaks and cascading waterfalls. Perhaps those of us brought up in less epic surroundings would have a better sense of *friluftsliv* should we too have called these imposing places home. Nevertheless, even the humblest of camping trips can connect us more acutely with the pleasure of Mother Nature – so pack that tent and sleeping bag and make your way into the wilderness to start your own *friluftsliv* lifestyle.

SABAI (สบาย)

/saɪ.baːjɨ/ | adjective | Thai

1. happy; comfortable; content

Our homes and environments can incite many emotions within us, but
one of the top feelings we tend to seek from our environment is comfort.
Enter the wonderful multi-purpose Thai word for comfortable, happy
contentedness: *sabai*. The Thai people use this term regularly. It even
forms the basis of that most everyday of greetings, 'how are you?' (*sabai
dee mái?*) and response, 'I'm fine, thank you' (*sabai dee kòrp-kOOn*). Yet
there are infinitely more ways in which this word is used – all of which
illustrate the relaxed and happy way of life that characterises
the Thai people.

A phrase often heard is *sabai sabai*, where the repetition adds
emphasis to suggest that something is very comfortable, often describing
a relaxing environment. In a person's home you may hear the invitation
to *nang sabai*, meaning 'sit and make yourself comfortable'. A pleasant
breeze would be *yen sabai*, or 'comfortably cool'. A cat that has found
a cosy spot to sleep within the basket of a parked motorcycle could be

described as *lap sabai*, meaning it is 'sleeping well' – and you are also likely to see this name given to hotels in Thailand, suggesting that they will offer a great night's sleep. Finally, the wonderful phrase *sabai jai* suggests a 'comfortable heart', and captures the absolute contentment we might feel when, for example, swinging in a hammock on one of Thailand's beautiful beaches.

For the Thai people, the *sabai* approach to life forms part of their cultural identity. While they are a diligent and hard-working nation, it is rare that you will see a Thai person rushing or stressed (as we imagine the typical Western working day to be). While Westerners tend to prize busyness as having a certain social status, the Thai people typically feel that, even while working, a more optimal state of being is *sabai* – tranquil and contented.

Given the Western tendency towards anxious and fraught lifestyles – resulting in an increasing search for alternative wisdom, such as mindfulness, to calm and centre us – the concept of *sabai* is a great word to add to our happiness vocabulary. Although we may not have the Thai beach life, we can all avoid rushing, create more relaxed environments – even at work – and treasure tranquillity. Why not make your day as *sabai sabai* as possible?

HUĀNYÍNG (欢迎)

/huan ŋɣiæŋ/ | exclamation | Mandarin Chinese
1. Welcome; 'to meet with joy'

Around the world, we have many words for welcoming people happily into our homes – few are lovelier than this Mandarin expression of welcome, at its most beautiful when amalgamated into the everyday greeting *huānyíng guānglín* (欢迎光临). While this entire phrase is often unimaginatively translated simply to mean 'welcome', it is far more nuanced than this. Formed of two character pairs, the first *huānyíng* literally means something like 'I meet you with joy', while *guānglín* can mean presence or 'light comes in'. So a more literal and difficult translation of *huānyíng guānglín* is the suggestion of a guest's arrival being as though light enters through an open door.

This beautiful imagery reveres a guest's arrival as an occasion, and shares some similarity with the English expression that a person can 'light up a room' with their presence. When we adopt *huānyíng guānglín* as a greeting, every person that enters our space is blessed with this term of endearment. Thus this commonplace expression – often heard spoken by the proprietors of shops and restaurants – is a heart-warming metaphor for the sensation of arriving into an environment where we feel welcomed and our presence is recognised as positive.

Although in China *huānyíng guānglín* likely falls into the category of phrases in daily life that are said often and yet rarely sincerely meant, there is nevertheless a lesson for all of us in its beautiful imagery. To be truly, ceremoniously welcomed into a space can be rare. How many of us can say we treat those we greet into our homes with the appreciation we would give to warm sunlight through the window?

While we might not feel this positively about every guest that appears on our doorstep – such as the door-to-door salesman or nosy neighbour – when loved ones do arrive, couldn't we all show our appreciation a little better? If you really want your guests to feel welcome in your home, then beyond offering a warm drink or comfy chair, try greeting them with the spirit of *huānyíng guānglín* – and let them know the light they have brought into your space simply with their presence.

Chapter Two

Community & Relationships

The happiest times of our lives are not usually spent in isolation, but among others: friends, family and loved ones of all descriptions. The best bits of human existence are communal: we laugh together around the dinner table or in the pub on a Friday night. We love together, and we treasure life's most precious miracles together at special ceremonies like weddings, celebratory holidays, festivals and concerts.

Equally, when times are hard, so too do we find encouragement, hope and optimism in the support of others. Well-being is an interconnected and truly collective experience. In fact, some psychologists have dubbed the sense of belonging – whether in an intimate relationship or a wider community – as the most far-reaching and integral factor in understanding human motivation and happiness.

All over the world, our differing languages articulate this fundamental nature of communities and relationships to our happiness, demonstrating how sharing, compassion and reciprocity underpin what it means to be truly well. Let us journey once again around the globe in search of a few more stamps in our happiness passport, and discover how the power of our bonds with others makes happiness, not only sustainable, but possible.

UBUNTU

ʊˈbʊntʊ | noun | Nguni Bantu

1. a common bond of unanimity between all people

None of us successfully become individuals capable of feeling true happiness without one very important ingredient: other people. Our early survival is entirely dependent upon the compassion, support and communication of caring others. Our identities, and even our very lives are, quite literally, given to us by others. Enter a word, therefore, that both clarifies and celebrates the significance of this human reciprocity, originating in the South African Bantu languages of Zulu and Xhosa: *ubuntu*.

Ubuntu is not only a word but also a philosophy. In Europe, and the West more generally, it is typical to think of 'me' as something singular, but across Africa the individual has traditionally been defined, not as flying solo, but as inseparable from the wider community.

Many African countries have their own unique interpretations of a similar concept. In Kenya there is the Swahili phrase *tuko pamoja*, meaning 'we are together', while in Tanzania you may hear *ujamaa*, Swahili for 'familyhood'.

The spirit of *ubuntu* philosophy is that only if something is good for the community at large can it possibly be good for the individual. This is an idea that is almost alien to the Western mindset, yet is perhaps more important than ever. Given our pressing environmental crisis, the inherent harmony of *ubuntu* seems like a powerful philosophy that is long overdue on the global stage.

When we talk about happiness, it is all-too-easy for this conversation to neglect the happiness – and harmony – of everyone. However, can we truly be happy while we know that others suffer and struggle? The happiness of everyone is of course an enormous task, and not one to be tackled overnight. Yet it is an idea worth carrying with us as we quest for greater well-being – so that perhaps we may one day be able to say: I am happy because we are happy.

GUNNEN

'yən.ən | verb | Dutch

1. to think someone deserves something; to derive
    satisfaction from someone else's success.

What's the quickest and most sure-fire way to make another person happy? Generosity. And, if you have ever visited the Netherlands, you will know the Dutch people to be some of the most generous and forthcoming that you can meet. Pause to look at your tourist map in Amsterdam and you may just find, rather than the derision and sneers you are likely to receive from locals in sprawling capitals like London or Paris, a local wanders over completely of their own accord to ask if you need help. Which brings us to a word that characterises this Dutch generosity of spirit: *gunnen*, describing the action of wishing a positive experience upon another, particularly in instances where the experience was earned, and even when their positive experience might deny us the same experience.

Gunnen, therefore, is a bit like the opposite of the English words 'begrudge' or 'envy' and closer to words like 'allow' or 'grant' – although these do not truly capture the nuances of the term. It also evokes the English expression that we give someone 'the benefit of the doubt' – and so describes a trusting, charitable and, perhaps at times, even self-sacrificing action.

Whether it is kindly giving someone directions, letting another person take first place in a queue or serving out the biggest portion at mealtimes to someone other than us, *gunnen* evokes the sort of selfless kindness that, if received, can change the whole trajectory of your day for the better. In fact, psychologists have shown that when we experience the kindness of another person, it can increase the likeliness that we will behave more kindly towards others ourselves – creating a domino effect to *gunnen*. Yet the kindness that *gunnen* characterises is not just good for others around us, but for us too. Performing kind acts correlates strongly with our own positive mood – with even a one-time generous action having potential benefits. With *gunnen*, everybody wins.

LIME

lʌɪm | verb | Trinidadian Creole

1. to party or hang out, usually in a public place with friends, sharing food, drinks and conversation; the art of idling

Anybody who has had the pleasure of spending time in the Caribbean will know the relaxed and easy way of life that typifies this uniquely laidback cluster of islands. One word that captures this with beautiful precision is the notion of *liming* - something you will hear daily among friends on the islands of Trinidad and Tobago.

Sharing similarities with the English concept of 'chilling out', yet with a unique Caribbean twist all its own, to *lime* is a fundamentally social activity. This is a shot of leisurely relaxation, with a dash of fun, mixed up with those we care about.

Liming will always involve at least one or two buddies, and should have no specific purpose other than its own: to unwind, chitchat, share some food or drink and just *be*. It is therefore an important backbone of friendships and communities across Trinidad - lying at the heart of many

social occasions from after-work drinks, to weekend plans, to the always-anticipated carnival season.

If you are invited to *lime* with Trinidadians on their beloved island then do not hesitate, for this word turns communal kicking-back into an art form. Perhaps you will share a beer or rum on the beach at Maracas Bay, listen to Soca (the lovechild of Soul and Calypso music) or chow down on any number of Trini delicacies, including 'doubles' (two round flatbreads heaped with a chickpea curry) and 'bake and shark' (fried bread filled with shark meat, salads and various sauces).

The origin of the word *lime* in this context is disputed, but a typical explanation is that, simply, one has nothing more pressing to do than relax under a lime tree. *Liming* is not attributed to any one age group or class of person, but is a widely shared cultural practice, valued by Trinidadians collectively. The Trini people take pride in their ability to let loose – and rightly so, because they are often some of the most good-natured and tranquil people you will meet.

So, the next time you make plans with friends, rather than planning a strict regimen of activities, put *liming* on the agenda instead and embrace this art of reciprocal repose.

ASABIYYAH (عصبيّة)

a.sa.ˈbiːja | noun | Arabic

1. community spirit; social cohesion

Happiness among a collective is something of an elusive concept to gauge. Individual happiness is easy to spot in sincere smiles and joyful words, but what is it that makes groups *happy* – from the smallest of nomadic societies to the grandest of empires? And, perhaps more vitally, what is that invisible glue that unites them towards a cause greater than the sum of its parts? The Arabic word *asabiyyah* evokes this collective spirit, which fuses us together even through the toughest of times.

Arabic is the sacred language of the Islamic faith, spoken by over three hundred million people worldwide. It may be of little surprise, then, that within this enchanting language we find a word describing that intangible, shared devotion that holds communities together in pursuit of a shared aspiration. *Asabiyyah* evokes social solidarity, unanimity and collective purpose verging on a shared group consciousness.

Asabiyyah is likely to be something we feel most strongly at political rallies or at celebratory national occasions, such as the marriage

of a monarch. In a sense then, *asabiyyah* is what our leaders rely on us having so that we do not descend into anarchy – a loyalty that is beneficial for all of us if it means we get along, but that might mean our compliance with the questionable choices of these leaders. Yet the community bond of *asabiyyah* can work on many levels – and therefore it may in turn be what leads some societies to work together to overturn governments that are no longer representative of the people. This is because *asabiyyah*, on the grand scale of civilisations as a whole, can be thought of as cyclical – most powerfully felt at the early forging-together of groups, then gradually waning, and eventually being usurped by a more appealing *asabiyyah*.

If we think of this in terms of community happiness, it is actually a rather heartening idea: that, at times, one form of *asabiyyah* or social solidarity serves us, but once it does not, it can be replaced. This is worth keeping in mind during even the harshest of political climates. *Asabiyyah*, just like individual happiness, is not static but cyclical, and therefore is always being revised and updated by its participants. If a set of circumstances is not truly making us happy as a wider community, then a new, revolutionary kind of *asabiyyah* may be a key ingredient for change.

VERSTEHEN

fɛɛˈʃteːən | noun | German

1. understanding
2. (Sociology) deeply empathic understanding of the behaviour of others, or putting yourself in another's shoes

A great deal of human unhappiness arises when we fail to 'see eye to eye', or we misunderstand each other. If only there was a rational and well thought-out method of comprehending the behaviour of others ... Well, funnily enough, there is – *verstehen* – and trust the ever-practical German people to have been the ones to come up with it. This is not simply understanding from a distance, but evokes the English expression that we put ourselves in another's shoes: we attempt to see someone's behaviour from their own perspective. *Verstehen* can therefore be literally translated as to 'understand', 'get', or 'see' – yet this is a small word that has sparked a much bigger system of sociological thinking, and one which has had philosophers pondering, for many decades, how humans might ever truly fathom one another.

The philosophy of *verstehen* suggests that, through engaged conversations and interactions, we might be granted a greater insight into the true motivations, perceptions and ideals of another person. Whether or not it is ever possible to fully understand another person – given that we cannot ever truly step into their shoes – *verstehen* is nevertheless a concept that can help us to think more profoundly about where others may be coming from on a given topic (much like *empathy* in English). Humans are usually happiest when they get along, and what better way to do this than by spending a little more time consciously trying to contemplate one another on an increasingly deep and meaningful level.

For you, *verstehen* might mean listening more attentively to your partner or a business colleague at those strained moments when you are perhaps failing to 'get' one another. It may mean taking the time to closely ponder and attempt to engage with the perspective of another culture, group or religion – despite the fact that their practices may differ greatly, even uncomfortably, from your own. While we are almost all guilty of enjoying the sound of our own voice a little too much, *verstehen* is a great reminder of the happiness and deep connection to be found when we stop, listen and try to truly understand.

Better together
on caring and connection

Humans put considerable effort into caring for one another – and it tends to pay off. The value of our bonds and connections is what psychologists call 'social capital' – the network of generous reciprocity between others and us. How do we create these precious networks? In Ireland, *bothántaíocht* means calling on neighbours to catch up on local gossip, while in Hawaii *ho'oponopono* is a practice of forgiveness in order to create greater connections and to rejuvenate relationships. We also form caring romantic bonds, as captured by *cafuné* from Brazil, or 'to adoringly run your fingers through a lover's hair'. Our dependence on those we love is expressed in the Arabic *ya'aburnee* meaning 'may you bury me' – a term of endearment articulating the hope that a loved one will die before us because we could not live without them. *Sneha* (स्नेह) is a Sanskrit word meaning both 'affection' and 'oil', evoking how our care can be applied to others like a balm, either literally as in Ayurvedic massage, or more metaphorically. In Japan, *amae* (甘え) describes a childlike surrendering to the care of another, while in Yiddish *nakhes* (נחת) is the affectionate pleasure a parent feels at their child's achievements, however minor. Where would we be without these treasured connections? Well, we would probably feel *awumbuk* (from Papua New Guinea), the empty sensation that comes over us after guests leave.

MELMASTIA (مېلمستيا)

mal'mæs.tia | noun | Pashto
1. hospitality and profound respect to all visitors regardless of race, religion or economic status, without hope of anything in return

The happiness of the Pashtun people of Afghanistan and Pakistan is formed from a selection of cherished virtues that, over time, have come to form a collective cultural code of ethics – perhaps unsurprising in a mountainous land that for many hundreds of years eluded any formal government or rule. This way of life is referred to as *pashtunwali* – a set of customs on how best to live, still followed by Pashtuns today. This code includes qualities such as justice, self-respect and tolerance – but also revenge (not one of the happier features of *pashtunwali*). Perhaps one of the most prized features of this code is *melmastia* – the practice of indiscriminate and profoundly generous hospitality to others, even complete strangers.

This tradition by Pashtuns to warmly welcome their guests – and even protect them should they be, for example, fleeing from an encroaching enemy – is a matter of great personal pride, and one that is still held up by many in modern times. It is a custom epitomised in proverbs passed down through generations, such as 'a guest is God's blessing' or that 'the guest is the ward of the host'. Many tribal villages may even have traditionally had a dedicated guesthouse where visitors to the village could find food and shelter – although this practice has declined as more modern, materialistic values have begun to reach even these secluded communities.

Nevertheless, the *melmastia* trait of heavy-duty hospitality is still alive and well for the Pashtuns, and is something from which we could all stand to learn a thing or two. As many of us around the world now live in increasingly secular cultures and communities, lacking guiding principles of times gone by such as to love our neighbour, we can be at risk of leading increasingly insular and distrustful existences. Many of us who live in apartment blocks may barely even know our neighbours. Yet, for a social animal like the human being, this is at odds with thousands of years of roaming the Earth in tribes. If we could all open our homes, and hearts, a little more – in the true spirit of *melmastia* – we may just find our well-being, and that of our guest (even if it's only that person you keep passing in the hallway), would get a big boost.

KANYININPA

kæn.jin'in.pə | verb | Australian Aboriginal (Pintupi)

1. holding; keeping

Humans tend to express their love and care for each other in one very overt and evident way: touch. Everything from hugs between friends, to kisses between lovers, to a mother holding her baby – all of these gestures illustrate how we express our feelings for others, not only with our words, but also physically with our bodies.

In fact, few things make us happier than touch – our brain literally produces feel-good chemicals in response to cuddles, caresses and cradling – and this is as true for city-dwellers as it is for desert-dwellers, such as the indigenous Pintupi people of Western Australia. Yet, in the Pintupi language, the word *kanyininpa* evokes a far wider significance and reverence for the concept of 'holding' that few other languages can rival.

Kanyininpa is deeply rooted in Pintupi values, and can be spoken in many contexts with various inferences. Arguably the most beautiful

of these, however, implies the delicate dynamic of respectful intimacy between those 'holding' and those being 'held'. This can apply on a small scale to a mother and her child or, on a far larger scale, to the elders in a community nurturing their young people. In fact, *kanyininpa* balances two poles of human experience that we can find in virtually all communities around the world – that of individual autonomy versus communal belonging, and the tension between these elements.

The literal and metaphorical implications of *kanyininpa* – holding and being held – illustrate the delicate balance to be struck between an individual and their community. The older generations of any society, in providing care and teachings to the younger generation, affirm this gentle equilibrium – and it is this dynamic that is felt to be at the heart of a healthy Pintupi community. Just as a mother holds, feeds and nurtures her baby, a society holds and nurtures its individual participants.

The spirit of *kanyininpa*, a value held dear by some of the most mistreated indigenous peoples in the world's history, serves as a reminder that even cultures so apparently different from our own possess the same essential values. Perhaps these shared values – of love and community – might now lead us, collectively, towards a kinder and markedly more respectful future.

PAASAM (பாசம்)

'pa:sʌm/ | noun | Tamil

1. affection

If there is one emotion that bonds human beings like no other, it is love. For those of us lucky enough to have experienced deep love, the notion of being intricately and tenderly 'tied' to the object of our affections is not a difficult metaphor to grasp. Even when we are not bound by genealogy, human beings create powerful attachments to one another that can be felt across great distances, survive tragedies and perpetuate for many years – perhaps, if we are lucky, even a lifetime. It is often these profound relationships that, above all else, bring us our truest experiences of happiness. This concept of deeply affectionate bonds between individuals is evoked by the Tamil word *paasam*, linked with the Sanskrit word *paasam* (पस) meaning 'tether'.

You could say that this notion of being tethered together with those we love is somewhat similar to the less-than-flattering English phrase that our romantic partner is our 'ball and chain' – something bound to our very being. Gratefully, however, *paasam* in Tamil has far more kindly connotations than this, evoking warmth and connection rather than duty and burden.

Yet the concept of *paasam* is not only reserved for the bond between lovers, and actually has far grander connotations and associations. In Shivaism – a major tradition within the Hindu religion that is primarily practised in the south of India – all souls are bound together by *paasam*, and both these souls and the powerful force of *paasam* that binds them, are under the control of *Pathy*, the Supreme Being, forming a trinity.

Whether or not your particular spiritual beliefs embrace these principles, it is hard to argue the kinship around which human life on Earth revolves. From the smallest of communities – perhaps even just two lovers – to the grandest of cities, nations, continents or religious groups that transcend these geographic borders, we seem to have as great a proclivity for union as we do for creating arbitrary divisions. Let us choose to place our focus on the former – that special *paasam* that ties us together, rather than what differentiates us.

GIGIL

'gʰiː,gil: | adjective | Philippine Tagalog
1. an overwhelming feeling, often in the context of
   wanting to pinch a cute or cherished baby

Sometimes happiness bursts out of us involuntarily, so that others can see exactly how we are feeling. Like any of our other emotions – fear, embarrassment or sadness – joy is an emotion that has its own repertoire of physical responses. Yet rather than trembling, blushing or tears – joy provokes grins, chuckles and sometimes even what the Tagalog language of the Philippines refers to as *gigil* moments. We have all been there. An adorable puppy is sat patiently outside a shop and, suddenly, we are filled with the pressing desire to grab it, squeeze it and never let go – often accompanied by strange high-pitched cooing sounds. Cherished babies and children are also typical inciters of that *gigil* feeling. Most of us will remember – much to our dismay – the *gigil* cheek-pinches from our aunts or grandparents when we were small.

Gigil experiences often relate to something thrilling, cute, enticing and which tests our powers of restraint – and if you are lucky enough to know anyone from the Philippines you will see how this word reflects their affable and light-hearted characters. However, it is worth noting that *gigil* moments come in other shapes and sizes too – ones that are not always so overtly positive. In fact, the word might loosely translate as 'frustration', or that teeth-gritting physical sensation when we see something that overthrows our usual ability to keep cool – which might mean something annoying.

However, we can think of the positive incarnation of *gigil* as just one item (in a list of many) that illustrates the worldwide human inclination towards care, compassion and just plain old good-naturedness. We love tiny things that require our care – sometimes to the point, as in the Philippines, of squealing outlandishly and squeezing them within an inch of their lives. At the heart of many of our relationships and communities is this *gigil* urge to connect physically and emotionally with others – be that a human or a four-legged friend.

Perhaps it is chubby babies that give you the positive *gigil* feeling, or perhaps it is puppies. Maybe you have even adopted a vegan diet because of your love of *gigil*-promoting piglets and curious calves. Whatever provokes *gigil* in you, next time you feel it, you will know precisely what to call it.

UNIKKAAQATIGIINNIQ

uːniːkaːkraːtiːdʒiːniːk | verb | Inuit (Inuktitut)

1. the power of story-telling and the role of stories in communal ways of being

Sometimes, what bonds happy societies is something illusive and indefinable – a certain spirit that is tricky to characterise and that we cannot quite put into words. Yet, often this bond operates precisely through words: stories.

For the Inuit people – the indigenous residents of the Arctic territories of Canada, Alaska and Greenland – there is a word that captures the important role of stories and story-telling in their way of life: *unikkaaqatigiinniq*. Through this concept, we can see the revered nature of stories as a way of sharing knowledge and of teaching everybody within a given Inuit community – both young and old – about the complexities of the world and potential ways of dealing with life's ups and downs.

The practical power of stories to impact our happiness is something we can see very plainly in the day-to-day life of almost any human culture and community you can think of. Story and myth have always played a vital role for human beings in creating shared morals, aspirations and instructions for living well. Indeed, the concept of happiness itself is a story, because it is one that differs from culture to culture.

When we collectively laugh, cry or even become deeply motivated by a certain story – this is the power of *unikkaaqatigiinniq*. This word speaks to the centrality of stories and oral-history to indigenous societies and their knowledge; allowing community members to express deeply held feelings and emotions without danger of breaking cultural limitations of discretion and humility.

Take a quick pause to consider the role that stories play in your own culture. From simple parables to the most outrageous of fictional tales – stories both bind and bolster us for life in the 'real world'. In fact, some psychologists have called fiction a simulation of real life, where we road test certain theories about human behaviour through 'what if' scenarios. How do you think *unikkaaqatigiinniq* plays a role in your happiness and the well-being of your community?

Chapter Three

Character & Soul

One of the principal ways that humans have pondered how to live well is through the idea of developing good character. The ancient Greek philosophers, for example, were big on this idea. Aristotle believed that possessing good character was not only about having an honest temperament, but about performing virtuous actions – and he often mused how closely happiness and character were linked.

All around the globe, we still spend a great deal of time contemplating this topic. There are more self-development books published every year; more blogs typed, advice penned and podcasts recorded on this subject than perhaps any other. This is quite heart-warming. We don't just want any old brand of superficial happiness: most of us want to be good people, too.

Unsurprisingly then, across our many languages we have developed numerous words that articulate how we become the most positive version of ourselves – whether this is through finding our ultimate purpose, through being courageous or through having compassion for others. Let's hop in our proverbial jet plane and take a quick zip around the globe in search of wisdom on how developing good character might make us happier.

SENY

/ˈsɜɲ/ | noun | Catalan
1. Sense; common sense (also integrity)

At times we are made happy by pure indulgence, the feeding of our impulses and wanton frivolity. However, most of us would agree that a deeper joy tends to arise from those moments in life where we have measured our actions, worked hard to achieve a goal and made ourselves proud. Enter *seny*, a custom originating in Catalan rural life, which loosely translates as 'good sense' yet has a far more layered meaning, including individual integrity, level-headedness and even self-realisation.

This word is felt by many to illustrate something specific about Catalan people and their culture. *Seny* suggests carefully considered actions, virtuousness and even perceptiveness – qualities still championed today by many Catalans who feel they continue to carry the torch of *seny* passed down the ancestral line.

Traditionally, the Catalans are a rational and practical people – and it is still easy to see this today as a foundation of their culture. A beguiling mix of being cautious while also impassioned about fairness and justice – if you are lucky enough to have a Catalan friend, you will know their advice to be sound and well thought out.

There are many parables and folktales illustrating *seny*, all of which champion wisdom and self-regulation, and eschew greed and excess. In one such tale, a peckish rat sneaks into a birdcage, but upon devouring the bird finds he is too fat to make his escape back through the bars.

In modern culture, where we can order pizza to our door and movies on demand, the idea that we should keep our greed in check seems woefully out-dated. Yet the superficial fulfilment of our appetites does not tend to make us happy for very long. Just like the gluttonous little rat, sometimes we can find ourselves having satisfied one desire at the expense of something we wanted much more – be that a healthy body, educated mind or meaningful relationship. Next time you spot yourself absent-mindedly tapping on your phone for a quick-fix takeaway or trashy movie, consider exercising a little *seny* instead. Prepare a wholesome meal from scratch or crack the spine of one of those books you have been meaning to read. It might just make you happier in the long run.

SISU

'siːsu | noun | Finnish

1. strength of will; courage; grit

Some cultures have a word they take so seriously that it shines almost as a national emblem. For the people of Finland, this word is *sisu*. Widely regarded as illustrating something very specific about Finns and their way of being, *sisu* evokes living with passionate courage even when the odds may be against us.

Few of us would argue that true well-being is ever possible without a strong dose of resilience. Life, as we all know first hand, has its challenges – and very often happiness is not naïve optimism in ignoring these challenges, but a positive determination to thrive despite them. This idea – that we should strive to have the courage to overcome adversity, even when the odds seem insurmountable – is captured by *sisu*. This little word evokes a superlative strength of will, or unwavering grit in pursuit of a long-term goal, perhaps with many obstacles.

The term also has similarities with the vaguely gruesome English phrase that a person has 'guts' or is 'gutsy', to mean that they are brave. This is because *sisu* in Finnish means 'interior' or 'guts'. *Sisu* therefore illustrates the stamina we are often able to draw on in crises, not from any exterior source, but from deep within ourselves.

Our own internal strength of character, or self-motivating ability when things aren't going as they should, is what French philosopher and writer Albert Camus once famously referred to as the steadfast summer to be found within the self, even in the darkest of winters – whether that may be a literal or metaphorical winter. Camus was reflecting on how we can each surprise ourselves with the immense inner strength we possess, to push back against that which life may throw at us.

Thus the notion of unswerving courage or *sisu* is perhaps one of the most important factors in the pursuit of a happy life. Happiness can be easy when things outside us are going well, but it is only when our tenacity is tested that we discover the true nuances of personal well-being. Happiness, after all, cannot be called true happiness unless it survives a few setbacks.

IKIGAI (生き甲斐)

i:ki:gai: | noun | Japanese

1. a reason for being; the joy and goal of living

There is a saying that the purpose of life is for our lives to have purpose, and in no other word for well-being is this idea better illustrated than in the Japanese *ikigai*, which suggests 'a reason to wake up in the morning'.

For the Japanese, everyone possesses *ikigai* – a word that combines *iki* (生き) meaning 'life' or 'alive', and *kai* (甲斐), which roughly suggests 'the realisation of what one hopes for'. Yet despite us all having *ikigai*, finding ours may entail much soul-searching.

This word can refer either to a certain something that makes our life meaningful (our family might be our *ikigai*, or a particular goal or dream we want to pursue), or it can simply describe the *feeling* that life has purpose. Sharing similarities, then, with the French term *raison d'être* (meaning the most important reason for one's existence), *ikigai* highlights a human ideal to be found the world over: the idea that we each need something in our lives for which it is worth rolling out of bed.

We might find the feeling of *ikigai* in our careers, but by no means is work the only place where one's ultimate purpose resides. Our *ikigai* might just as easily be our children, partner, friends, creative passion or charity work. Some Japanese people would say that *ikigai* is a far more lofty notion than the everyday purpose of work or family – and that only the greatest poets or even saints could be said to truly have *ikigai*. Nevertheless, here is a word that can prompt all of us to examine exactly what is at the heart of our enthusiasm for existence.

Can you readily point out your *ikigai*, or is this sense of deep purpose an ideal for which you are still fervently searching? Many of us probably fall into the latter category so do not fret if this includes you. *Ikigai* can be seen, not as something static, but as a gradual process of blossoming into our innate potential.

Good advice

**Happy sayings
about living well**

One way that we pass wisdom through the ages for building character and living well is in our expressions and sayings – and it is fascinating how these differ around the globe. The Ukrainian language could teach us all a thing or two about working too hard. They have a saying describing how we can easily pick up a task again later: *robota ne vovk, v lis ne vtiče* (робота не вовк, в ліс не втіче), or 'work is not a wolf, it doesn't run into the woods'. In Hungarian, were you to be feeling downtrodden by life, you might be told *úgy szép az élet, ha zajlik*: 'life is beautiful if it is happening' – a reminder that when times are hard it can be helpful to focus on your gratitude just for being alive at all. If this doesn't make you feel better, someone may cheer you up in Ireland by advising: *is maith an scéalaí an aimsir*, or 'time is a good story teller', to help you see that things may make sense in the long-term. If you need a bit more general encouragement to get moving, in English you may be told to 'shake a leg', while a Czech person would tell you *pohnout kostrou*, literally 'to move one's skeleton'. Should you then feel better and recover some vitality and energy, in English this might make you feel 'fresh as a daisy', whereas in Spanish you would feel *fresco como una lechuga* or 'fresh as a lettuce'.

MERAKI (μεράκι)

ma'ræ.ki: | verb | Greek
1. to do something with soul, or from the heart

As rational beings, many of our actions have great practical purpose. We do certain things to get a job done, to fulfill a logical outcome or to achieve a result. Yet a lot of the things we do as humans do not come from this rational, cerebral part of us at all, but from another place entirely – what we sometimes colloquially call actions 'from the heart'. Which brings us to the Greek verb *meraki*, loosely meaning actions infused with our passion. *Meraki* evokes activities that are performed with a certain ardour and creativity – things done with loving devotion to the task. This might include anything from dancing to decorating our home with ardent attention and care – *meraki* can also imply having 'good taste'.

With this term, the Greek language depicts how we can all leave a little part of ourselves in even the most everyday of creative actions – perhaps just lovingly preparing a coffee for someone. *Meraki* illustrates how we are often motivated, not by our logic, but what we call our soul. If a friend were coming over for lunch, it would probably make sense to prepare something quick, simple and nourishing – yet perhaps we remember that thing they really love to eat, and so we spend two hours preparing a deliciously involved feast and arranging the dinner table with our best place mats and fresh flowers. Thus, what could have been the humblest of lunches is now infused with our love and passion, reflecting a little more of our own inner essence than a quick round of sandwiches ever could. This is *meraki*.

Unsurprisingly, the word is applied to many artistic pursuits – music, singing, painting, writing – any activity where we have skill, engage our whole hearts and into which we invest our enthusiasm. The Greeks are exemplary *meraklides* (people possessing *meraki*), demonstrated in everything from their beautiful homes, to their lively music and merry-making, to their deliciously colourful fresh food. Let us learn from them and make like a *meraklis* (male) or *meraklou* (female) – a person who squeezes joy from every moment and who lives with zest.

MENTSH (מענטש)

mɛntʃ | noun | Yiddish

1. a human being
2. an honourable person

Happiness is rarely tied to one single element or feature of our lives. We are not usually happy only because of our environment, or only because of our friends, or only because of our successes – happiness is a juicy fruit salad of all of these aspects of life. Equally, then, having good character is not usually about possessing one single positive trait, but is rather a whole gamut of good things rolled into one. Which brings us to the important and multi-dimensional Yiddish concept of being a *mentsh* – a word that originates from the German *mensch* (where it simply means 'person'), and which has also become a loanword in American English.

In Yiddish, to be a *mentsh* evokes being an admirable human being – someone others trust, respect and look up to. This might include being just, dignified, humanitarian, compassionate, generous, a 'stand up guy' or someone revered and even emulated by others. Collectively,

these many positive traits make up *mentshlekhkeyt* (מענטשלעכקייט), the attributes of a *mentsh*.

We often describe this idea of possessing a variety of positive traits as being someone who is 'well-rounded'. Having a balanced character is prized because, as human beings, we do not usually aspire only to be good colleagues or dedicated worker bees – we also want to be good friends, good sons or daughters, good citizens, good neighbours. Thus, being a *mentsh* is not simply about achieving status or wealth, or having a revered job title. This word has nothing to do with our level of worldly success. To be a true *mentsh* runs much deeper than material assets or what we are on paper – it is about living our lives kindly, charitably and in a way that draws profound respect from others, not simply for what we are, but who we are. Let this word prompt you to consider your own strengths and qualities as a *mentsh* – and serve as a reminder that material success is just one measure of many when it comes to truly living well.

ĀTMAN (आत्मन्)

/'aːtmən/ | noun | Sanskrit

1. the true self or soul
2. breath

Most of us have the sense of having a 'real me' inside of us, whether or not that is what we always show to the outside world. In fact, when it comes to our individual happiness, it is precisely this true inner self that we tend to talk about. This idea – that deep within each of us there exists an essential self – is one that has kept philosophers in both the East and the West arguing for many centuries. One thread in this vastly rich tapestry of philosophical debate is the Sanskrit word for soul, *ātman*, which brings to light a very particular conception of self.

In the Hindu faith there are some diverging avenues of thought surrounding the *ātman*, yet it can be broadly considered to be the beating heart at the centre of our existence as human beings. *Ātman* refers to the eternal, fundamental self, running far deeper than the ego and existing beyond any false shades of self we may project.

This notion of the self as eternal supports a spiritual belief with which we will almost all be familiar: the concept of reincarnation, or that one soul may inhabit multiple temporary bodies. In fact, we may even say that, rather than material beings having occasional spiritual experiences, a human being can be better defined as an eternal spirit, the *ātman*, having an earthly, bodily experience.

However, we need not necessarily share the deeply spiritual beliefs surrounding the *ātman* in order to derive wisdom from this term. The poignant dual meaning of this word as both 'soul' and 'breath' reminds us of two utterly vital yet overlooked aspects of happiness in our fraught modern lives: to breathe and to reconnect with a certain steady permanence within ourselves. So much of our lives – and our selves – exist in a bewildering flux. Our emotions change like the weather. The roles we adopt shift with the regularity of the daily news. To counter this force, a practice such as meditation or yoga can help us to become better acquainted with our own *ātman* – that reliable, beating rhythm at the centre of our existence, as vital and fundamental as our breath gently inhaling and exhaling.

ARRANGIARSI

a.ranˈdʒaːsi: | reflexive verb | Italian
1. to make do; to get by with one's own ingenuity

Happiness sometimes befalls us as the result of good luck. On these occasions, wonderful sets of circumstances pop up out of the blue, with little-to-no direct effort on our part, and we simply get to sit back and luxuriate in these windfalls. At other times, happiness is hard-won. At these times we scrape together whatever limited means we have at our disposal, and simply make the best of the situation.

When it comes to this kind of resourcefulness, few cultures can compete with the Italians. Italy is the birthplace of some of the world's most beloved art, music, literature, architecture and of course, food – highlighting what these wonderfully spirited, feisty and generous people can achieve when they put their minds to it.

One uniquely Italian term that may be at the heart of this enterprise and tenacity, and which encapsulates this spirit of resourcefulness, is the reflexive verb *arrangiarsi*. Literally translating as 'to arrange oneself', the

connotation of *arrangiarsi* evokes doggedly adapting oneself to one's circumstances – even those that are challenging. Yet this is not merely a throwaway term, but a true way of life for many Italians. Indeed, getting by is a well-practised art form, captured in the common phrase *l'arte di arrangiarsi*, or 'the art of getting by'. This saying signifies the personal skill and creativity required to survive and thrive even on limited means.

If anything represents *l'arte di arrangiarsi* in Italy it is their magician-like ability with preparing delicious food from minimal ingredients. Particularly in the south of the country, a place historically plagued by poverty, taking fresh local ingredients and transforming them into veritable feasts – and a cuisine loved the world over today – evokes the true spirit of *arrangiarsi*. A somewhat similar concept is found in the Portuguese *desenrascanço*, the ability to 'disentangle' oneself from a tricky situation by finding an artful solution to the problem.

To bring a little of *l'arte di arrangiarsi* into one's life is no mean feat. It requires adaptability and seeing creative solutions instead of obstacles – something that is, understandably, not a gift we can all possess, all of the time. Yet *arrangiarsi* is an empowering concept to keep in mind when it comes to happiness – gently reminding us of the perpetual human drive to adapt and thrive, even in adverse situations.

YĂNG SHĒNG (養生)

jæŋ ʃəŋ | verb | Mandarin Chinese
1. nourishing life; to keep in good health

Happy, healthy longevity is something most of us aspire to in life. We wish to live lives that are long and full of vitality – not cut short or plagued by ill health. Indeed, having good character and being oneself are usually underpinned by a vital requirement: healthy bodies and minds. We can find it much harder – sometimes impossible – to live well and be at our best when we do not feel physically or mentally well. Unfortunately, however, good health is often an afterthought for many of us – only becoming important when we lose it. In traditional Chinese medicine, and consequently in Taoist philosophy, this is not the case – beautifully illustrated in the concept of *yăng shēng* meaning 'nourishing life'.

Yǎng shēng involves a system of daily practices, usually done by ourselves for own benefit, that, when combined, promote our well-being and reduce the impact of ageing. Underpinning *yǎng shēng* therefore is the philosophy that physical well-being is something we should nurture daily, just as we might water a pot plant – not only something to treat or pay attention to when illness arises.

Yǎng shēng includes good nutrition, as well as mind-body exercises that balance the energy within the body such as t'ai chi, qigong, meditation and other forms of breath work. Contemporary Western thought has also begun to recognise that such practices can be deeply nurturing and help to support us in being the healthiest version of ourselves – both mentally and physically.

How do you consciously nourish your own health and life force daily? Healthy habits are not always easy to form, but if we look at them in terms of *yǎng shēng* – as a nurturing practice for our health that promotes longevity – we may just be more encouraged to form them. Begin your own *yǎng shēng* practice today – you will surely feel the benefits.

FLAITHIÚIL

flæ'hu:l | adjective | Irish Gaelic

1. princely
2. munificent, lavish, generous

The notion of good character is a collectively sanctioned one: we decide as communities what a good member of that community looks like. Unsurprisingly then, around the world character traits geared towards the greater good are treasured. These include attributes such as kindness, compassion and generosity of spirit – caring characteristics that we all seek and expect to find in happy groups, neighbourhoods and cultures. Even in most Western cultures, which typically prize individual gain, we still revere this habit of altruism and looking out for others.

In Irish Gaelic, this idea is captured in the beautiful word *flaithiúil* (pronounced 'flahool'), which is also commonly used in the English spoken in Ireland. An adjective derived from *flaith* meaning 'prince' or 'lord', *flaithiúil* describes someone generous, magnanimous or noble in character.

While this word is evocative of Medieval times when land-rulers were expected to act generously, *flaithiúil* is a term that speaks to an enduring and endearing characteristic of Ireland as a nation – an exemplary generosity and readiness to give to those in need. Whether through helping a stranger, volunteering their time or donating money, the Irish people regularly rank as some of the most charitable in the world according to the World Giving Index. In fact, on more than one occasion Ireland has topped the charts as the most charitable country in Europe.

The lovely paradox of having a *flaithiúil* nature is that we can often feel most ourselves when we stop thinking about ourselves, and act in service to others. Most of us will have experienced the profound sense of happiness to be found through *flaithiúil* behaviour. This is because, as deeply social creatures, the sense of connection we feel in the giving and receiving of generosity is a central tenet to our well-being (and, historically, to our very survival). Ironically, therefore, when we feel down, often the best way to shake this off is through offering our time and energy to someone else – be that a friend or relative in need or even a total stranger. From simple acts like assisting a passer-by who has dropped some coins, to dropping a few of our own coins into the hands of someone less fortunate, we could all take a leaf out of Ireland's book and find daily ways of being more *flaithiúil*.

AHIṀSĀ (अहिंसा)

/əˈhɪmsaː/ | noun | Sanskrit

1. reverence and non-violence towards all sentient beings

There are many religious and spiritual concepts around the globe that teach us to live more ethically, more purposefully and, at their heart, more joyfully. Perhaps among the most beautiful of these is the concept of *ahiṃsā*, meaning, at its simplest, 'non-injury' or 'non-violence'.

Ahiṃsā is the foremost ethical principle of the Jain religion of India, while also being a cherished value within Hinduism and Buddhism – illustrating that there are some human ideals that transcend even religious borders. In Jainism, however, *ahiṃsā* is a guiding North Star against which all human actions should be judged.

Ahiṃsā does not imply pure passivity, but describes a kind of power that we exert when we act in kind service to all living beings. Literally translated, *ahiṃsā* means 'lacking any desire to kill', but what this means in practice is exemplified in a parable found in traditional Indian folklore. In the tale, a *sannyasi* (the title given to Hindu monks who have performed their own funeral and renounced social standing) happens upon a scorpion while sitting meditating at a riverbank. The scorpion has fallen from a tree and is struggling to stay afloat in the water. The *sannyasi* retrieves the scorpion and returns it to the tree but, before placing it down, is stung. Ignoring the injury, the *sannyasi* returns to his meditation. Some time later, the same scorpion falls into the water once again. The *sannyasi* assists once again, and is stung once again. This chain of events repeats several times before a passing villager notices the interaction and questions the *sannyasi*, exclaiming, 'why go on helping that rascal if he continues to bite you?' The *sannyasi* replies that 'it is in the scorpion's nature to sting, and he cannot help himself'. 'Why not simply avoid him?' asks the villager. The *sannyasi* answers, 'because I am a human being, I cannot help myself either; it is in my nature to save him'.

It is this spiritual practice – and indeed joy – of service and respect towards other living beings that is captured in *ahiṃsā*. This is something towards which we may all aspire, to play our part in a kinder and fairer planet.

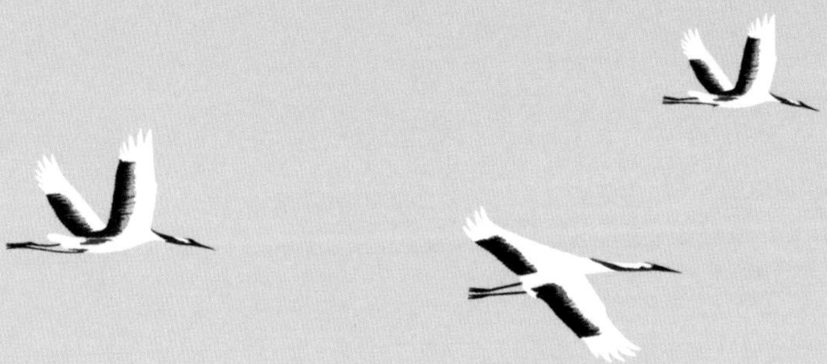

Chapter Four

Joy & Spirituality

Around the world we find plenty of ways of speaking about – and celebrating – life's crowning moments: the peaks of high spirits, merriment or mystical awe. Whether we talk about them in spiritual or more material terms, these moments can be personally transformative and incredibly special. We may only have a handful of these sublimely joyous times in our lives – but it is precisely their scarcity that makes them feel so miraculous.

Such occasions can spin the trajectory of our lives off in a completely new – and happier – direction. In fact, it is difficult to envision a truly happy life without them. They can range from the silly and light-hearted, to the serious and profound. Yet one thing that unites these joyful occurrences is the sense of self-transcendence they afford us: we lose ourselves in laughter, awe, compassion for others or a sense of spiritual alignment. This 'loss of self' in moments of joy or spirituality can be an incredibly positive and liberating thing, offering a sense of greater connection and purpose.

Let us now explore some of the diverse ways that we talk about joy and spirituality around the globe – and how our world's many languages capture and celebrate these great crests of human experience.

SERENDIPITY

ˌsɛr(ə)nˈdɪpɪti | noun | English

1. a fortunate or happy unplanned coincidence

It is likely that almost all of us will have experienced the feeling of a 'happy accident'. In these rare yet delightful instances the stars align and events transpire in a way that we could not possibly have orchestrated ourselves – with wonderfully positive results. In the English language these fortunate occurrences fall under the heading of 'serendipity', meaning a pleasant coincidence verging on the mystical. Serendipity evokes the sense of something being destined for us, perhaps in a grand universal plan.

Maybe someone offers to lend us a book on the exact topic about which we have recently become passionate. Or we miss our train only to get chatting with someone incredible on the later one. Or maybe we flunk a job interview only to be offered our dream job the next day. Serendipitous moments give us a sense of something being our fate – even if this is defined less by the idea of a pre-programmed plan for everyone, and more by the conviction that not everything in life is under our direct control (but will perhaps be more spectacular than even our best laid plans!).

The British art historian Horace Walpole is said to have coined the concept of serendipity several centuries ago. In a letter to an acquaintance he described crafting the word from a Persian fairy tale, *The Three Princes of Serendip*, in which the heroes make multiple, unintentional-yet-positive discoveries.

In the Western world, where we have traditionally defined ourselves as self-determining individuals each forging our own unique destiny in the world, the concept of serendipity is a useful reminder that we are not always in control of what happens, but that this does not have to be a bad thing. In fact, some psychologists such as Dan Gilbert have suggested humans are notoriously bad at predicting what will make us happy. What better reason, then, to embrace serendipity and invite a little positive coincidence into our lives – it may just make us happier than we ever could have planned.

YŪGEN (幽玄)

ˈjuːɡən | noun | Japanese

1. grace
2. something deeply profound or unfathomable

Some joyous experiences can stir feelings within us that are truly impossible to capture in words. Yet we can but try. Enter: *yūgen*, the Japanese word evoking how we feel when we encounter the profound and mysterious beauty of the universe. *Yūgen* is usually spurred by aesthetic splendour, particularly in the natural world. This word therefore shares some similarities with the English 'awe', which also describes the feeling of being deeply moved, sometimes even to tears, and often by grand natural landscapes.

We might experience *yūgen* as we wander through a park of cherry blossom trees, or in watching a pink sun sink behind snow-capped mountains, or in gazing wistfully at a formation of wild cranes flying overhead. An inexpressible, poignant sensation washes over us – one we cannot quite grasp or fully understand. Entirely evanescent yet intensely profound, these experiences can be personally transformative.

Originating in Chinese philosophy, *yūgen* highlights the Taoist concept of the purposelessness of nature – yet in the most positive sense. Most of us have hopefully experienced the idle, aimless sensation of sitting against a tree with nothing to do but pick at blades of grass for no reason at all; or of watching the summer sun dance on a river as we listen to the gentle lapping of water and hum of bees. In these moments, we abandon rationality for a moment and enter pure, harmonious experience. These are the instances where we realise our identity as human beings, and not human doings.

Sometimes these experiences are simply calm and peaceful, other times they are intensely moving when all of a sudden we recognise our incapacity to fully fathom or integrate within ourselves the magnificence of our universe. This is *yūgen*.

Yūgen is unlikely to be a feeling that we can schedule into our day planner – yet it is one that we could all almost certainly do with more of. And, sometimes, simply having a word for a feeling – even if it will only ever half capture it – can bring us closer to the experience. Try blocking out a couple of hours of 'aimless nature time' in your diary – preferably somewhere beautiful, and at sunset – and go in search of your own moment of *yūgen*.

DADIRRI

dəˈdɪ.ri | verb | Australian Aboriginal (Ngangikurungkurr)

1. deep listening; humble contemplation of one's place in nature

Indigenous to the Daly River region of Australia's Northern Territory are the Ngangikurungkurr people, and among these people we find the concept of *dadirri*. This word has been said to translate loosely as 'contemplation' – yet it appears to evoke something more than meditative thought and can be more accurately translated as 'inner deep listening' as well as 'quiet still awareness'. It is said to evoke a kind of spiritual tuning in – perhaps to each other, but also to nature – such as we might experience when sitting alone on a riverbank.

Thus *dadirri* seems to be less about productive pondering and more about a profoundly humble, receptive form of awareness of the world around us. When we listen with the spirit of *dadirri*, we become conscious of the depths of our inner world and our place in the wider landscape, in a way that may be personally fulfilling. More

than this, *dadirri* suggests respectful, quiet patience as the splendidly slow tread of our rivers and weather systems unfold (an idea that runs entirely counter to the typically busy and self-involved human agenda so associated with fraught city life).

For a culture such as the Ngangikurungkurr people, this reverent spiritual connection with the natural world is not surprising. In fact, the name Ngangikurungkurr itself evokes the natural world: *ngangi* means 'word' or 'sound', while *kuri* means 'water', and *kurr* means 'deep' – giving this tribe a name that implies 'deep water sounds'. For these individuals, as for many indigenous cultures through time, the land upon which they depend is sacred. Their reliance upon their environment is so pressing, and their attachment to it so evident in daily life, that it is no wonder we find concepts such as *dadirri*.

Dadirri articulates how spirituality necessitates our openness to a force mightier than us, be that Mother Nature, the wider Universe, or another more mystical force. Such humility is easily lost in modern, concrete cities—but it need not be lost entirely. Find a moment today to sit in quiet receptivity, in the spirit of *dadirri*, and simply listen to the world unfolding around you.

KEFI (ΚΈΦΙ)

'keə.fi | noun | Greek

1. high spirits; merriment; mojo; love of life

All of our emotions translate to certain physical expressions, yet joy is an emotion with some of the most beautiful examples. Moments of joy manifest in dance, song, laughter – we even jump for joy! This is something we can see across almost all of our human cultures, yet one place where the physical manifestation of joy is precisely captured in its very own word is in Greece. *Kefi* (κεφι) is a Greek word, which is tricky to translate but equates to something similar to 'high spirits' or 'merriment'.

If you have ever travelled to Greece you will know the particular flair with which this culture expresses its love of life, or *kefi*. On balmy summer evenings there is music, dancing, ouzo drinking, plate smashing and all manner of overt, exaggerated jubilation. *Kefi* evokes this deeply felt experience of enjoyment with wild abandon – where we are fully

engaged, cathartically, in a joyful physical expression of our positive inner spirits.

The experience of *kefi* is also a profoundly collective one. This is visually evidenced in traditional communal Greek folk dance, where interlocking arms and handholding unite the dancers. This kind of coordinated, carefree and exuberant movement is infused with *kefi*. Yet such moments of *kefi* are fleeting. These exulted experiences where we forget our woes for a while do not last forever – although perhaps it is their rarity that makes them so special.

An important element of *kefi* for the Greek people is to treasure these moments of positivity and exhilaration, even when times are tough. *Kefi* is a shared moment of elation, and it is precisely these moments that bond us socially with one another. When we consider that social bonds are one of the most important psychological factors to our well-being, it seems like the Greeks are on to something with their cherishing of *kefi* as a way to face unpleasant circumstances. It is through strong, close bonds with others that we are perhaps most likely to overcome such circumstances, and this is exactly what *kefi* gives us.

WHIMSY

'wɪmzi | noun | English
1.   playfully quaint or fanciful behaviour or humour

Like most cultures, the people of Britain express joy through their own particular and unique sense of humour. One shade of this is captured in the curiously untranslatable word *whimsy*. This distinctive English term can mean anything from imaginative to quirky to cute to comical – and is in fact a peculiar blend of all of these. *Whimsical* things make Brits happy, perhaps because they balance an otherwise stern and serious culture. Think of Mary Poppins, the magical nanny who brings laughter and *whimsy* to the household of an austere Edwardian family.

To be *whimsical* is to be light-hearted, fancy-free and perhaps make very little sense – and so it is a descriptive word that can apply in many situations. A typical British teashop, for example, might be *whimsical* in its decoration if it had quirky mismatched china, bright floral wallpaper, bunting and framed embroidery.

A person may also show a lot of *whimsy* through their characteristics or even appearance. Perhaps they will have a witty or amusing way of looking at the world (think of the strange, *whimsical* characters that Alice meets when she falls down the rabbit hole into Wonderland). A person may also dress *whimsically* if they choose bold colours or eccentric combinations of patterns and styles.

Whimsy is essentially about frivolousness and not taking life too seriously. It is therefore common for mythological storybook characters, such as fairies and elves, to often be associated with the word, due to their mischievous, fantastical and ephemeral natures.

Try bringing a little sprinkling of *whimsy* into your world by doing one thing daily that is utterly silly, fanciful or nonsensical – for no reason at all other than it is delightful, daring or amusing to you. So much of our lives are spent in a serious race to some far-off finish line of success, status or achievement – it is no wonder we are often left feeling fatigued. A little bit of *whimsical* triviality every now and again can be the perfect escapist flight of fancy to counter this trend – and to bring a bit more light-hearted joy to our lives.

Dinner at ours

The joy of food around the world

If we humans find pleasure and joy in one pastime above (virtually) all others, it is eating. How we talk about this delightful activity, however, varies across our many languages. In Georgia, *shemomedjamo* is a term for continuing to eat even when full, because your meal is so delicious. The drowsiness we may feel after doing so is captured in the Italian *abbiocco*. After food often comes caffeine, as in the Greek *Parea* (Παρέα), which refers to a group of friends who meet regularly to socialise over coffee and swap stories of their lives, values and philosophies. Similarly, in Sweden, *fika* is a word for taking a break for coffee and pastries. If you decide to move from coffee to alcohol, the Catalan *porrón* might come in handy – a peculiar jug with a long spout used for drinking wine. In Turkish, *çakırkeyif* is a word for the joy of the drinking person who has not yet lost lucidity (similar to the English *tipsy*). And what of food etiquette? In Persian culture, *taarof* is the complex set of manners that surround our acceptance of the hospitality of another person, such as an acquaintance asking you to stay for dinner in their home. The art of *taarof* would dictate that you decline and be persuaded several times in order to establish whether the offer is genuine or mere politeness. More informal meals have words all their own: in Icelandic, *álegg* is a multi-purpose noun for anything that you might put on bread (jam, meat, cheese), similar to the English *toppings* for things we put on pizza. Now, who's hungry?

BON VIVANT

bõ vivã | noun | French

1. literally 'person living well'; a person committed to a luxurious, sociable life

Our character is often so intimately tied to our culture that it can be difficult to unpick which begins where. This idea takes us to France – the land of good wine, great romance and Parisian chic – where we find a term for a certain kind of character that embodies a love of the most splendid things in life: the *bon vivant*. Literally meaning 'person who lives well', this term has become commonplace in the English language, perhaps because it describes a person we all know. Picture a *bon vivant* and you may envisage a stylishly dressed individual, sipping champagne and hosting a dinner party for their many fabulous friends.

Some may call the life of the *bon vivant* shallow. Yet rejoicing in life's pleasures is not a mere symptom of the superficiality of modern life, but is a practice we can trace back to Ancient Greece and the notion of *hedonism*. This philosophical theory – derived from the Greek *hēdonē* meaning 'pleasure' – holds that pleasure-seeking and pain avoidance are the principal forms of human happiness, and therefore that fulfilment of such desires is a justifiable life goal. Whether or not you agree with this philosophy, there is no denying the mood-boost we can all feel when we indulge ourselves a little.

Interestingly, in contemporary psychology, happiness is often referred to in two senses: *hedonic* to refer to pleasure-seeking, and *eudaimonic* to refer to those experiences that may not be immediately pleasurable but hold a deeper meaning for us, such as pursuing education or raising a family. Therefore it is worth noting that both of these types of experiences usually combine to make life happy. Whether or not, like the true *bon vivant*, your life is full of glitzy soirees and champagne sipping, we may all benefit from a little dash of hedonic happiness in our day-to-day, even if it's simply a luxurious bubble bath, glass of wine or delicious dessert. Let us learn from the French people and savour life's little indulgences – perhaps not as our ultimate goal, but as pieces in the patchwork of a life lived well.

DUYÊN PHẬN

zwiən˧˩ fən˧˩ˀ˩ʔ | noun | Vietnamese

1. fate in love

We will nearly all have had this experience of meeting, as we dub it in English, a *soulmate*. This is a beautiful concept that can refer to either a romantic relationship or special friendship. The word *soulmate* evokes a person so fantastically like ourselves and so attuned with our worldview that it feels like a miracle to have crossed their path. Even if we hold no other spiritual beliefs at all, we might say that the meeting was 'written in the stars' or that we are 'kindred spirits'. We have the overwhelming feeling that it was our destiny to know this person – or we may even get the eerie, superstitious sense of having already known them for a long time.

In Vietnam, this same sense of fated spiritual kinship with other individuals is taken very seriously, and captured in the term *duyên phận*. This concept evokes the predestined or fateful feeling of affinity we can experience when we meet treasured others – be they our friends or a romantic partner. In this sense, *duyên phận* is akin to the happy accident evoked by the English *serendipity* (see page 92), or the well-known Buddhist concept of *karma*, yet differs in that it relates specifically to fortunately fated relationships.

As Vietnam has been so heavily influenced by Chinese culture, it is perhaps no surprise that *duyên phận* is a concept that links with Chinese philosophy, specifically the notion of *yuanfen* (緣分), which similarly evokes the predestined nature of our close relationships. This is beautifully evoked in the Mandarin expression that 'it may take a hundred reincarnations for two people to ride the same boat, but it takes eons for two people to share the same pillow'.

Duyên phận highlights how many of our most elevated, joyful and spiritual experiences are the result of meeting cherished others. For most of us, the entire trajectory of our lives seems to hinge on the fact that we crossed paths with a handful of special people – it is little wonder, then, that these relationships can often feel like fate, or *duyên phận*. These are the friendships and love affairs where we feel the sense that it was truly 'meant to be' – and imagining life without those people is practically impossible.

JOIE DE VIVRE

ʒwad vIvʀ | noun | French

1. exuberant enjoyment of life

In France, joy is not merely an emotion, it is also an attitude, a worldview ... you could even call it a philosophy to live by. This lust for the jubilantly lived life is encompassed in what these continental Europeans dub *joie de vivre* – literally, 'joy of living'. This special phrase denotes a person's zest and enthusiasm for existence – and has long captured the hearts of English-speakers who have embraced the expression into their own language.

Something that makes this turn of phrase so poignantly French is its recognition that the purpose of life need not always be practicality, but passion – and if there is one thing that France gets right, it is passion. This is the country that gave us the 'French kiss' after all.

Joie de vivre is less about having a pragmatic reason for your life, and more about getting a kick out of the journey, just ... because. Picture *Amelie* elatedly eating raspberries from her fingertips and you will have the perfect image of *joie de vivre*.

The French have a knack for putting *joie de vivre* into their everyday. We can express *joie de vivre* through enjoyment of food – and the French certainly do so with an unbridled devotion to their cuisine, internationally recognised as one of the finest in the world. For the French, even a meal as practical as breakfast becomes a delectably indulgent affair – just think of a warm *brioche* or *pain au chocolat*.

Perhaps, for you, your *joie de vivre* emerges through an engaging artistic hobby, through travel, through romance or through any activity where you feel yourself to be fully engaged in the delights of life.

The important thing about *joie de vivre* is that it is a way of being – not a set of circumstances we await. Experiencing and savouring joy in life are active experiences, not passive ones. If anything, then, living with *joie de vivre* is a practice – and one that we can begin at any time. It is always our choice to celebrate the little things, rather than treating joy as a rare peak experience reserved for birthdays or wedding days.

Celebrate being alive today, and express a little *joie de vivre* yourself.

MURĀQABA (مراقبة)

murəkəbe | noun | Arabic (from Sufism)

1. to watch over; to take care of
2. heightened awareness of one's spiritual heart through meditation

All of the world's religions have developed their own specific spiritual practices – not only for worship but also for improving personal well-being. Of these, meditation is one practice that has become increasingly common around the world, even among the non-religious. The ancient, mystical religion of Sufism maintains its own particular form of this spiritual practice, and this is captured in the term *murāqaba* – a kind of watchful self-care that we achieve through meditation.

An important prerequisite to *murāqaba* is *muḥāsabah* – a process of self-accounting, or self-inventory. This is a regular practice, perhaps daily, of examining one's actions, motivations and achievements in the world. In *muḥāsabah* practice we may ponder: why have we behaved the way we have? What was the outcome? What did we fail to achieve? Are we satisfied with these actions, and do they align with our highest aspirations?

In performing *muḥāsabah* and thus 'taking stock' of the self, the Sufi tradition holds that we positively develop our relationship with the divine. Through this practice, we become increasingly watchful (*rāqaba*) and aware of the influence of the divine. Thus, through continual *muḥāsabah* self-inventory and *murāqaba* meditation, we may eventually enter a state of *mushāhada* – a witnessing of the presence of the divine in one's own heart.

While these are sacred spiritual practices that form part of a vast constellation of religious beliefs and practices within Sufism and, more broadly, Islam, such spiritual ideals can shed an interesting light on all of our lives, even if we are non-religious. In fact, modern cognitive scientists have begun to unpick how different forms of the spiritual practice of meditation may not only support calm well-being, but even change our brains in different ways – and, in turn, affect our very selves. This research is only just beginning, so findings are as yet unclear – however it highlights a fascinating and constructive meeting point between spirituality and science, illustrating how the wisdom of ancient religions may continue to support us, even if our beliefs diverge.

UKI-OKTON

uːgiːʊədgɒn | noun pair | Haudenosaunee (Iroquoian)

1. the balance of positive and negative spiritual energy present in humans and nature

Today we understand that concepts like happiness, when examined across cultures, are not straightforward. We are fascinated by the subtle and untranslatable nature of certain words or phrases, perhaps precisely because of this modern-day humility about our broad diversities. We know that there are delicate, sometimes un-graspable nuances to be duly acknowledged. Historically, however, this humility has not existed to the same extent, and some concepts have therefore entered our lexicon quite skewed from their original.

Such seems to be the case with the Haudenosaunee (or Iroquoian) concept of *uki-okton*. The singular concept of *uki* – loosely meaning a positive spiritual energy found in both humans and nature – is often described individually using another term: *orenda*. Yet today some argue that *orenda* captures only one half of the complex and gracefully balanced beliefs of these indigenous peoples, better encompassed in the dual term of *uki-okton*.

In speaking of *uki-okton*, the positive spirit energy of *uki* is balanced by the more negative spirit of *okton*. Yet neither *uki* nor *okton* is inherently good or evil, but simply … *is* – reminding us that, within all of nature, nothing is black and white. This idea is similar to the widely known Chinese philosophical concept of *yīnyáng*, literally meaning 'dark-bright', or 'positive-negative', and highlighting how seemingly conflicting forces are usually interconnected. In Haudenosaunee myth, the two twins – *uki* (or Sapling) and *okton* (or Flint) – both offer help to humans and cause havoc for them respectively. This illustrates the balance of certainty and uncertainty in nature, and therefore in human life.

We might say, then, that if *uki-okton* is present in all things, then it is in our own moral actions that we can choose to emphasise the positive. This idea is echoed in the folklore of another indigenous North American people, the Cherokee. Here we find the legend of a wise grandfather imparting advice to his grandson, where he explains that within everyone there exists a struggle between a 'good wolf' characterising benevolence, kindness and justice, and a 'bad wolf' signifying greed, envy and superiority. The grandson asks curiously, 'but, grandfather – which wolf will win?' to which he is told, 'the one you feed'.

Chapter Five

Balance & Calm

Just like in nature, human life possesses a certain ebb and flow, wax and wane, bloom and wilt. While our emotional life may have joyous peaks, if we look at happiness as something overarching, then we see that it must necessarily have many shades – we cannot expect ourselves to always be 'up'.

In the English language we cherish 'downtime' – a word used to describe the periods when a machine is switched off, and therefore describing times when we free ourselves from work and activity and simply relax. Most of us understand that such peaceful 'down' moments are essential to our well-being. We know that both our emotional and physical health demand a delicate symmetry between eventful action and serene rest. Achieving equilibrium between these states is what we often refer to as being balanced. The way we interpret this across cultures, however, illustrates an intricately varied mosaic of experiences.

From the perfectly practical (such as the special Danish brand of work-life balance), to the profound (as in the Chinese philosophy of letting nature take its course), let us circle the Earth now for words capturing this special human capacity to counter life's peak moments with a little bit of sensible balance, rejuvenation and serenity.

LAGOM

'là:gɔm | adverb | Swedish

1. just the right amount

We all know the very specific unhappiness of scarcity, as well as the discomfort of excess – and for this reason we can all grasp the particular joy, à la Goldilocks and the Three Bears, when something is *just right*. Cue the Swedish term that sums up this special kind of balanced bliss, and which typifies a nation of sensible and tolerant individuals: *lagom*.

   Said to represent an alternative view to greedy consumerism, *lagom* is a term linked with everything from how much cake to eat, to the temperature of a room, all the way up to environmental sustainability – suggesting there is always a perfect amount to any experience, and an amount we would be well advised not to exceed. It is therefore a word that brings to mind modesty and shrewdness, encompassed in the typical Swedish phrase *lagom är bäst*, meaning literally 'the right amount is best', but also sometimes translated to mean that there is virtue in moderation.

For many of us, it is rare that we link well-being simply with sufficiency. We tend to associate peak happiness with being 'rich', achieving 'abundance' and circumstances that are 'plentiful' or even 'lavish'. Yet the truth is that lavish experiences only fill us with joy for as long as they are novel. Most of us will return to baseline happiness even after the most major of windfalls. This idea – known in psychology as 'hedonic adaptation' or the 'hedonic treadmill' – highlights how our desire for 'more, more, more' is perpetual. Even though we trick ourselves into thinking our appetite may one day feel fulfilled, there is always something else to lust for. What better evidence could there be for the importance of a concept like *lagom*?

We can all make choices that are a little more *lagom* and reap the positive benefits of doing so. Chiefly: embracing a level-headed contentment that counteracts the insatiable hunger of our consumer-driven world. Whether this is making modest meals with simple ingredients that avoid waste, or in striking that hallowed work-life balance between busyness and relaxation, *lagom* is a way of life where we choose to value adequacy over extremity, and thus a satisfied happiness over frenzied accumulation.

AJURNAMAT

a:jɜːnæmæt | expression | Inuit (Inuktitut)

1. calm acceptance when something cannot be helped or is out of one's control

A great many of our less-than-happy moments arise when we frantically attempt to control something that is beyond our power to change. In the influential 'Serenity Prayer' – a short and well-known mantra often used in rehabilitation programmes – we ask to be granted the serenity to accept the things we cannot control, the courage to change what we can and the wisdom to know the difference. This illustrates a profoundly simple yet challenging philosophy to live by – and one that can often mean the difference between our happiness and unhappiness.

A word that captures this philosophy beautifully is *ajurnamat* (also spelt *ayurnamat*), found in the Inuktitut language – one of the foremost Inuit languages of the Canadian Arctic. *Ajurnamat* is a word uttered in response to circumstances – even extremely trying and difficult circumstances – that simply cannot be helped. From the smallest mishap to the greatest of tragedies, *ajurnamat* is about not heaping extra suffering on ourselves by believing we can change what we cannot. This serenity in the face of hardship is not an easy trait to master – and is therefore something for which the Western world has developed an increasing hunger.

It is unsurprising to find such a word among a people who have long survived in some of the harshest weather conditions on Earth. In fact, *ajurnamat* evokes a trait we find in many indigenous cultures that have lived closely connected to nature: the idea of humility and reverence for the changing tones and temperaments of the natural world, as opposed to an imagined dominance over nature.

Can we still thrive when we cease to imagine ourselves in control of everything? The answer is an unequivocal *yes*. The reason for this is that control is so often an illusion – when we trick ourselves into believing that we are the master of all things then we are simply setting ourselves up for a fall. This applies across a vast range of human experience, from indigenous survival, to the city-dwelling bride who believes she can craft the perfect wedding day, but then it rains. Is rain on your wedding day simply one-nil to Mother Nature, or is it a chance to practise *ajurnamat*, put on your wellies and celebrate with a splash? The choice is always yours.

SÓLARFRÍ

ˈsɔːlaˌfriː | noun | Icelandic

1. an unexpected day off from work because the weather is fine

Any of us who have lived the 'nine-to-five' lifestyle will understand that occasional (or frequent) sensation first thing on a Monday, where nothing would make us happier than an extra day to ourselves. This is especially true when weather conditions are particularly conducive to having a good time outdoors, and not being stuck in an office. Picture the scene: you wake up to glorious morning sunshine, with barely a cloud in the sky ... and then realise with regret that you have to go to work. Wouldn't it be nice if employers the world over empathised with this conundrum and granted us all the day off when the weather is nice? Well, reportedly, Icelanders do just this, and even have a word for it: *sólarfrí*, which literally translates as 'sun' (*sólar*) 'holiday' (*frí*).

This joyous practice makes sense, really, in a subarctic climate that is notoriously unpredictable – and where the mean annual temperature

for the capital city of Reykjavik is just 5°C. If warm sunshine is a precious commodity, it is logical that the people of Iceland should make the most of it.

Sólarfrí captures a certain spirit of positive ingenuity that characterises Icelanders. These are a people who understand and revere their environment, but also know how to use it to their advantage. This is a nation that is only fractionally powered by fossil fuels – with the heating and hot water for most buildings provided by geothermal energy (hot volcanic water bubbling deep underground). What's more is that a substantial portion of Iceland's electricity is produced by renewable hydropower. This sustainable way of living in harmony with the natural world is just one of the many reasons why Icelanders rank as some of the happiest, healthiest people in the world.

Sólarfrí may not be a practice we will all be able to convince our bosses to adopt, but it is a good reminder to strike our own daily balance between working hard and making the most of our surroundings – even if this just means getting out into a green space on our lunch break to soak up some rays.

Fancy a stroll, sauna
or siesta?

**Ways we relax
around the world**

Modern-day psychologists tell us that the positive emotions we feel during our calmer, contented moments of relaxation can both fuel our resilience in tougher times, and unravel the lingering effects of stress, such as rapid heart rate and raised blood pressure. But this is nothing new – all of the world's major religious traditions from both the East and West have long prescribed calming and centring practices as a tool in living life well. Today there are many ways that we humans choose to relax around the globe. In Greece, you may go for a *volta* (βόλτα) – the traditional activity in small towns and villages of taking a stroll around the winding streets or shoreline at dusk (the French language has the verb *flâner* with a similar meaning). In the Nordic countries, a favourite way to unwind is to go for a collective sweat in a *sauna* – a small room of steam or hot air to refresh the body. The Finnish people are particularly committed to this practice, with virtually every home having one built in. In Spain, relaxation has traditionally been embedded into the workday via the infamous *siesta* – a long afternoon nap following lunch, when the sun is at its hottest. Even today, across Spain many shops and businesses will shut during this time. Whether a stroll, a good sweat or a quick nap takes your fancy, relaxation and leisure time are essential to our happiness wherever we live, so be sure to get your dose today.

WÚWÉI (無為)

wu:weɪ | verb | Traditional Chinese (from Taoism)
1. effortlessness; letting nature take its course

The Chinese philosophical concept of *wúwéi* – while it is often translated as something literally meaning non-doing, non-action or non-striving – has been described as a word that we might be better off not trying to translate at all. This is because *wúwéi* actually *is* a kind of doing, but, almost paradoxically, doing with absolute ease.

Wúwéi describes both a way of acting in the moment and a way of living life overall. It can be understood as a manner of effortlessness and harmony as we move through the world, while – importantly – being an effective individual. If you imagine a highly skilled musician playing the harp (or ancient Chinese *konghou*) and making it look easy – even effortless – then you have something close to *wúwéi*. Of course, playing the harp isn't easy for just anyone, but thousands of hours of practice have made this challenging activity a breeze for the player. The best translation of *wúwéi* might therefore be 'effortless action'.

Wúwéi has long been a spiritual ideal in Chinese philosophy, despite being an incredibly subtle art. How (or if) we can ever fully realise the *wúwéi* way of living is a wonderful mystery – hence the difficulty, and perhaps even futility, of trying to translate this word. Different strands of Chinese philosophical thought depict *wúwéi* as something hard-won through painstaking study and practice, or conversely as something intrinsically present in all of us. However *wúwéi* is achieved, and whether it forms a way of life or is reflected in our individual actions, most schools of thought agree that this term encompasses an intricate combination of skill, spontaneity, ease and enjoyment. Sounds pretty good, doesn't it?

We could all stand to be a little happier through living our lives the *wúwéi* way – especially if we think of it a little bit like a skilled and graceful brand of tranquillity, where we learn to act with artful effortlessness in our responses to life.

MAÑANA

/maˈɲana/ | adverb or noun | Spanish

1. tomorrow
2. an unspecified time in the future

We might describe the Spanish word *mañana* – which literally means 'tomorrow' or 'morning' if you put *la* in front of it – as the art of putting things off. While Spain is a culturally diverse country, there is something uniquely Spanish about this word in its positive-yet-relaxed philosophy. Across the many corners of this land one can find a certain shared light-heartedness towards living that *mañana* evokes. A Spaniard will surely come to your party – indeed, they will probably be the life and soul of it – but they may not show up on time.

This approach can be an incredibly calming attitude when it is practised with conviction (even if only every now and again). Ask yourself: what if I didn't worry about this today, what if I waited until *mañana*? Odds are you will feel instantly more relaxed.

In fact, the concept of *mañana* illustrates that, when it comes to happiness, it can be helpful to give up our iron grip on trying to expertly manage or organise our time. Very few things truly need to be done right now – and if we worry ourselves into oblivion thinking they do, or imagine that we will one day 'get ahead of ourselves' with all we have to do if we keep on working at a frenzied level, then all we end up doing is forever chasing our tail and mistaking it for productivity.

You probably already know someone who is an expert in this art of elusiveness: the kind of person who refuses to worry about things in this moment when it can be dealt with later. It is the attitude of 'why fret over this now, when tomorrow it may not matter anymore?' Take a leaf out of their book today and put a task (or two) off until *mañana*. When that distant point in time eventually does come, you may find it doesn't matter quite as much as you thought.

KEYIF

kɜ:u:θ | noun | Turkish

1. pleasurable state of relaxation and well-being

We often feel relaxation through a specified activity, but what of those times when we relax by doing precisely nothing? The Turkish people have a name for this: *keyif*, and those in the bustling city of Istanbul call it their secret weapon when it comes to well-being.

Keyif (sharing roots with the Greek word *kefi*, yet having a unique Turkish interpretation all of its own) can have many shades, making it difficult to translate; it evokes anything from enchantment, to delight, to euphoria, to tranquil relaxation. In Istanbul, *keyif* is often described as the art of quiet, blissful repose; an absorbed form of peaceful contentment. In this busy city, experiences of *keyif* are defined by doing absolutely nothing: simply sitting still, being fully present in the moment, perhaps while gazing out at the glistening water of the Bosporus.

Keyif is interesting when we consider that, typically, we seek *ways* to relax – we hunger for practices like yoga, meditation, walking, having a bath or reading to help us slow down and pause. Even when we are

not actively doing something and claim to be 'relaxing' with a coffee on our couch, our mind can still be a-buzz with thoughts of times gone by or things we are anxious about for the future. The Turkish *keyif* evokes the idea that we stop doing anything at all, both physically and mentally, enjoying the here and now without worries of the past or future.

In this sense, *keyif* echoes the concept of mindfulness – though it seems to lean more towards savouring the pleasure of the moment, rather than attaining pure awareness as mindfulness promotes. *Keyif* goes to show how, even in busy city life, we all treasure moments of peace and stillness.

Try it yourself. Become blissfully aware of the present moment, perhaps with your morning coffee; not simply letting go of your worries and becoming mindful, but luxuriating in the peaceful serenity of just ... sitting still, quietly, in peace. You may find you want to have all your morning coffees with a side of *keyif* from now on.

ARBEJDSGLÆDE

ɑːbaɪgskɪlɪ | noun | Danish

1. happiness in one's work

Until we reach the ripe old age of retirement, few of us are lucky enough to luxuriate in calm relaxation for the greater part of our days. What do we do instead? We work. How, then, do we achieve the hallowed 'work-life balance' in these busy periods of our lives? Does a hectic work schedule mean that for only a few short hours of an evening, or at the weekends, we are truly enjoying our lives? Not so if we embrace the Danish term *arbejdsglæde*, which means literally 'work gladness'.

The closest English translation of *arbejdsglæde* would probably be 'job satisfaction', but this humdrum phrase hardly radiates the same happy feelings. *Arbejdsglæde* illustrates a striking cultural phenomenon about Denmark, which is that Danes regularly rank as some of the happiest employees in the world. The reasons for this are not rocket science. In Denmark, holiday time is substantial and working hours are reasonable – with Danes working on average two hundred and fifty hours less per year than North Americans.

Yet less time at work is by no means the only reason why the Danish feel generally more content in their working lives. Another factor that has been suggested is the increased autonomy Danes feel at work (autonomy is often a primary factor to job satisfaction), due to less hierarchical relationships between bosses and their so-called subordinates. In Denmark, if your boss asks you to do something, it can be taken as more of a suggestion than a duty. This differs radically to, again, the workplace dynamic in North America – where the word 'boss' is vaguely synonymous with all-powerful.

Variants of *arbejdsglæde* exist across a number of Scandinavian languages – but before you pack up your briefcase and jump ship to Northern Europe, consider the fact that the Danish *expect* to enjoy their jobs. For many of us, 'hard' work is virtuous – suggesting that gainful employment is intrinsically a kind of drudgery. Consequently, enjoying our jobs somehow suggests a lack of work ethic. So, perhaps the real change required to achieve *arbejdsglæde* is not a geographical one, but scrutiny of our own preconceptions.

SEIJAKU (静寂)

,seɪ'dʒɐ.kə | noun | Japanese

1.   silence
2.   moments of tranquillity, even amid day-to-day activity

When it comes to balance, it is easy to get trapped in the 'if only ...' hypothesis. This is when we convince ourselves that contentment and calm will be ours 'if only' we could just achieve something else, go somewhere else or even be someone else. This idea is, of course, a kind of quicksand where the relaxed life sinks to its death. The uncomfortable reality is that we must often commit to finding serenity despite circumstances to the contrary – simply because we are the only ones to suffer if we do not. Enter the Japanese concept of *seijaku* (静寂), which describes the moments of peace to be found, not atop a quiet snowy mountain peak in some far-off future, but in the daily race of life.

Seijaku is one of seven principles in Japanese aesthetics and Zen philosophy that make up *wabi-sabi*. Originating in Buddhist philosophy, *wabi-sabi* is an appreciative worldview that accepts impermanence and embraces the beauty of imperfection. *Wabi-sabi* champions the unfinished, the asymmetrical and the austere. *Seijaku* is the feature of tranquillity within this set of principles, and is often described in terms of the sensation we experience when sitting in a peaceful Japanese Zen garden, even in the middle of a busy city like Tokyo. *Seijaku* is the feeling of peacefully escaping the crowds, noise and pollution for even just ten minutes, to soak up the serene atmosphere of koi ponds, decorative rock gardens and lofty bamboo.

Seijaku therefore captures how a little bit of tranquillity can be embedded within daily life, not heralded as some glittering Oz all the way at the other end of the Yellow Brick Road – available to us 'if only' we could eject ourselves from our reality entirely.

You may like to keep *seijaku* in mind next time you need to take five – whether it's from work, parenting pressures or something else – and commit to treasuring the little pockets of blissful tranquillity available to you, even amid the busy buzz of your day.

SOBREMESA

so.βre'me.sa | noun | Spanish

1. the period of relaxed conversation around the dinner table, following a meal

In much of Spain, lunch is an elaborate affair. Wherever you go you are likely to spot '*Menu del Dia*' (Menu of the Day) signs, which will include starter, main and a dessert, plus bread, wine and coffee – usually for a steal. This Mediterranean take on the midday meal (which actually commences at two or three o'clock) can last for several hours, and may even be followed by a snooze (a *siesta*) before going back to work in the evening. And you had better fill up – dinner may not be until ten o'clock at night.

One factor that makes Spanish meal times so languorous – aside from the balmy heat of the noon sun – is the concept of *sobremesa*. This word describes the time spent relaxing, chatting and digesting around the table immediately after a meal – and if you have ever experienced the cramping indigestion of rushing back to work after a hastily consumed sandwich on your feet at a counter, then it probably sounds quite appealing.

Sobremesa time typically lasts between half an hour to an hour but, in the evening or in summertime, may stretch on for several hours. This is a time that is both pleasant and practical: too much physical movement after a large lunch is likely to give anyone an upset gut, so the Spanish replace this with comfortable discussions and laughter instead.

These meandering Mediterranean meals could not be more dissimilar to the efficient half-hour lunch breaks in the UK and North America, where a clingfilm-wrapped snack at one's desk is a regular occurrence. Even in the evenings many of us tend to eat from our laps on the sofa while watching television - not even bothering to lay the table, let alone relax around the table post-feast.

Yet, with an increasing appreciation of focused and mindful activities to counter our stressful lives, what better way to develop such practices in the daily nooks and crannies of our lives than through more engaged meals? Try consciously taking the time after your next lunch or supper to sit and chat with friends and loved ones around the table in the spirit of *sobremesa* - because, really, why are we in such a hurry to clear the plates or pay the bill?

COCOG

tsoo.tsoog | noun and adjective | Javanese

1. to be in agreement
2. to match
3. congenial

In Javanese language – the dominant language on the Indonesian island of Java, and the native language of around sixty million of its inhabitants – balance and harmony are important. So important, in fact, that being in accord with both nature and one another has traditionally been something of a way of life for the Javanese people. This spirit is encompassed in the word cocog (also spelt cocok or tjotjog). If something 'fits' together in perfect accord, then it is cocog, and as long as things are cocog then everyone's happy – for this word describes instances as diverse as when a meal is delicious, to when a medicine effectively cures an ailment, to any number of other satisfying or agreeable circumstances.

Most of us would agree that it is particularly important for a marriage to be cocog; in other words, for the two partners to be a good match. To ensure this, the families of Javanese would-be-brides traditionally visit the graves of their ancestors to receive their blessing for the union (a couple that is not cocog is likely to divorce).

In fact, harmonious cocog interactions of all kinds are important to Javanese culture, and in day-to-day life on Java interpersonal conflict is usually avoided at all costs. So central is this peaceable harmony to the Javanese cultural identity that young children who have yet to learn to behave cordially – in the spirit of cocog – are sometimes dubbed durung jawa, or 'not yet Javanese'.

Few of us can claim to take harmony to heart as deeply as the Javanese, yet what if we were guided a little more by congruence in our daily lives? It seems as good a philosophy for happiness as any other. We might seek out a job or career that is a little more cocog. We might aspire to more cocog friendships. In choosing paint colours for our next decorating project we may ask, 'hmm, but is neon green really cocog in my home?' It seems that a life lived in this spirit of compatibility could be a very happy one indeed.

A Happily Ever After

This book has been a treasure hunt. In our joyful journey around the globe we have pieced together a story about what it means to be a happy human being – wherever we are from, whatever our environment, our upbringing, our spiritual beliefs or our lifestyle.

Words like these, and the stories we weave from them, have a remarkable knack for making us happier. Our lives can be complex and confusing. Often, the only way that we can make sense of them is through words and stories – told to others, and to ourselves. What is marvellous about this is that even when life becomes troubled we always have the ability to craft our own happy ever afters – through the alchemical art of storytelling.

Just like any story, ours has come to an end – we have arrived at a moment of *eucatastrophe*. This rare word in the English language illustrates a specific super power of stories – the uplifting sense of conclusion they can offer us. This is because *eucatastrophe* means the swift and favourable resolution of events in a narrative; what we more commonly call a happy ending, or happily ever after. The term was allegedly coined by the celebrated storyteller, J. R. R. Tolkien, and is drawn from the Greek *eu-* (good, or well) and *katastrophē* (overturning, or sudden turn).

Eucatastrophe is just one example of how words create our world. Words serve to console and to guide us, like little compasses, in the great journey of living well. So allow the terms within these pages to expand your imagination as you pen the next chapter in the story of your happiness, and let them remind us all of the part we have to play in narrating a happier world – word-by-word.

Extend the Journey

You can find out a little more about the words included in this book, as well as the psychology behind them, with these further resources.

ʻĀina
Wood, A.M., Froh, J.J. and Geraghty, A.W. "Gratitude and well-being: A review and theoretical integration." *Clinical psychology review*, vol. 30, no. 7, 2010, pp.890-905.

The great outdoors
Cervinka, Renate, Kathrin Röderer, and Elisabeth Hefler. "Are nature lovers happy? On various indicators of well-being and connectedness with nature." *Journal of Health Psychology*, vol. 17, no. 3, 2012, pp.379-388.

Prostor
Berdahl, D., Bunzl, M. and Lampland, M. eds., *Altering States: Ethnographies of transition in Eastern Europe and the former Soviet Union*. University of Michigan Press, 2000, pp.190–191.

Waldeinsamkeit
Emerson, Ralph Waldo, "Nature." *American Transcendentalism Web*, https://archive.vcu.edu/english/engweb/transcendentalism/authors/emerson/nature.html

Friluftsliv
Gelter, H. "Friluftsliv: The Scandinavian philosophy of outdoor life." *Canadian Journal of Environmental Education (CJEE)*, vol. 5, no. 1, 2000, pp.77-92.

Huānyíng
Milazzo, J. "10 Chinese Words with No English Equivalent." *TutorMing Mandarin Learning Tips Blog*, http://blog.tutorming.com/mandarin-chinese-learning-tips/chinese-phrases-that-cant-be-translated

Community and Relationships
Baumeister, R. F., & Leary, M. R. "The need to belong: Desire for interpersonal attachments as a fundamental human motivation." *Psychological bulletin*, vol. 117, no. 3, 1995, pp.497-529.

Ubuntu
Nussbaum, B. "Ubuntu: Reflections of a South African on our common humanity." *Reflections: The SoL Journal*, vol. 4, no. 4, 2003, pp.21-26.

Gunnen
Pressman, S.D., Kraft, T.L. and Cross, M.P. "It's good to do good and receive good: The impact of a 'pay it forward' style kindness intervention on giver and receiver well-being." *The Journal of Positive Psychology*, vol. 10, no. 4, 2015, pp.293-302.

Better Together
Kreuter, Marshall W., and Nicole Lezin. "Social capital theory". *Emerging Theories in Health Promotion Practice and Research: Strategies for improving public health*, vol. 15, 2002, pp.228-254.

Kanyininpa
McCoy, B.F. *Holding men: Kanyirninpa and the health of Aboriginal men*. Aboriginal Studies Press, 2008.

Paasam

Kanagasuntheram, R. "Science and symbolism in Saivaism." *Aum Muruga Journal*, vol. 21. 2003.

Unikkaaqatigiinniq

Healey, G. and Tagak Sr, A. "Piliriqatigiinniq 'Working in a collaborative way for the common good': A perspective on the space where health research methodology and Inuit epistemology come together." *International Journal of Critical Indigenous Studies*, vol. 7, 2014, pp.1-14.

Mar, R.A. and Oatley, K., "The function of fiction is the abstraction and simulation of social experience." *Perspectives on Psychological Science*, vol. 3, no. 3, 2008, pp.173-192.

Sisu

Lomas, T. "Towards a positive cross-cultural lexicography: Enriching our emotional landscape through 216 'untranslatable' words pertaining to well-being." *The Journal of Positive Psychology*, vol. 11, no. 5, 2016, p.19.

Ikigai

Mathews, G. *What makes life worth living? How Japanese and Americans make sense of their worlds.* University of California Press, 1996, pp.12-13.

Meraki

Tsounis, D. Kefi and Meraki "Rebetika Music of Adelaide: Cultural Constructions of Passion and Expression and Their Link with the Homeland." *Yearbook for Traditional Music*, vol. 27, 1995, pp.90-103.

Mentsh

Rosten, L. *The New Joys of Yiddish.* Crown Publishing, 2003, pp.232-233.

Ãtman

Flood, G. "Hindu Concepts." *BBC.co.uk*, http://www.bbc.co.uk/religion/religions/hinduism/concepts/concepts_1.shtml

Yâng shēng

Wilcox, L. "Nourishing Life (養生 Yâng Shēng): An Ancient Love of Lists." *Journal of Chinese Medicine*, vol. 113, 2017, pp. 28-31.

Ahiṃsā

Britannica Encyclopedia of World Religions. Encyclopædia Britannica, 2006, p. 24.

Serendipity

Gilbert, Dan, *Stumbling on Happiness*, Vintage, 2007.

Yūgen

Watts, Alan, *The Tao Of Philosophy*, Tuttle Publishing, 1999.

Dadirri

Ungunmerr, M. R. "To be listened to in her teaching: Dadirri: Inner Deep Listening and Quiet Still Awareness." *EarthSong Journal: Perspectives in Ecology, Spirituality and Education*, vol. 3, no. 4, 2017, pp.14-15.

Kefi

Pattakos, A. "'Opa!' The Cathartic Value of Greek Dance." *Huffington Post*, https://www.huffingtonpost.com/alex-pattakos/dance_b_882612.html

Maios, T. "Kei: A Greek Word that Can't be Translated." *Neo Komo*, http://neoskosmos.com/news/en/%CE%9AEFI-a-Greek-word-that-cant-be-translated

Bon vivant

Ryan, R.M. and Deci, E.L. "On happiness and human potentials: A review of research on hedonic and eudaimonic well-being." *Annual Review of Psychology*, vol. 52, no. 1, 2001, pp.141-166.

Murāqaba

Lobel, Diana. *A Sufi-Jewish Dialogue: Philosophy and Mysticism in Bahya Ibn Paquda's Duties of the Heart*, University of Pennsylvania Press, 2006, pp.224-226.

Dahl, C.J., Lutz, A. and Davidson, R.J. "Reconstructing and deconstructing the self: cognitive mechanisms in meditation practice." *Trends in Cognitive sciences*, vol. 19, no. 9, 2015, pp.515-523.

Uki-okton

Johansen B. E., and Mann B. A. *Encyclopedia of the Haudenosaunee (Iroquois)*, Greenwood Publishing Group, 2000, pp. 83, 231-233.

Ajurnamat

Leduc, Jean, "Bearing Witness." *Maclean's*, vol. 112, 1999.

Wúwéi

Barrett, N.F. "Wuwei and Flow: Comparative reflections on spirituality, transcendence, and skill in the Zhuangzi." *Philosophy East and West*, vol. 61, no. 4, 2011, pp.679-706.

Arbejdsglæde

Kjerulf, Alexander, "5 Simple Office Policies That Make Danish Workers Way More Happy Than Americans", *Fast Company*, 2014. https://www.fastcompany.com/3029110/5-simple-office-policies-that-make-danish-workers-way-more-happy-than-americans

Cocog

Geertz, Clifford, *The Religion of Java*, University of Chicago Press, 1976, p. 31.

ABOUT THE AUTHOR

Megan C Hayes is an author and academic and has spent a decade studying and researching writing and the psychology of happiness. Megan's interdisciplinary PhD explored writing as a tool to promote and support psychological wellbeing, and she has shared her research in the UK, USA, and Europe, including papers in *The International Journal of Wellbeing* and *Writing in Practice: The Journal of Creative Writing Research*. From this research Megan pioneered the Positive Journal® approach to personal writing (www.positivejournal.org)—a way to put wellbeing into words. She is a happy wayfarer who calls the globe home, but wherever she is she can usually be found drinking tea and reading five books at once.

ABOUT THE ILLUSTRATOR

Yelena Bryksenkova was born in St Petersburg, Russia, grew up in Cleveland, and studied illustration at the Maryland Institute College of Art in Baltimore and the Academy of Arts, Architecture and Design in Prague, Czech Republic. Now living in Los Angeles, Yelena works as a fine artist and illustrator for clients such as Anthropologie, Chronicle Books, *Flow* Magazine and *The New York Times*. Her pen and acryla gouache paintings are inspired by her love of home and the comfort of everyday objects, as well as more magical, mysterious and melancholy themes.

THANKS

I am grateful to Philippa Wilkinson for having a fantastic idea for a book, and for inviting me to write it—with thanks also due to my agent, Jane Graham Maw, for making the connection. Thanks to the wider team at Quarto for your vital and varied cultural insights, and Yelena for your splendid illustrations. Lauren Gurteen, I am especially thankful to you— my generous friend and linguist extraordinaire—for deciphering the pronunciations of some of the more obscure words here. Ramesh Sivarajah, thank you for your suggestion of the Tamil *paasam*, and for reading through my attempt at capturing it. Kathleen Tompsett, thank you for your friendship, hosting of me in Buenos Aires as I wrote this book, and for introducing me to the wonderful intricacies of Trini culture since 2010, so that I could include our favourite pastime, *liming*, here. Thank you to Gwen Healey at the Qaujigiartiit Health Research Centre for your informative advice with the two Inuktitut words found here, I only hope I have done them some justice. Thank you also to Barbara Alice Mann for your emails regarding *uki-okton*, which I would not have any kind of pronunciation for without your help! Thank you, Tim Lomas, for your continuing work in this vital area. Your timely research on "The Happy Words Project" is a unique and invaluable resource for us all. I am thankful as always for my family, my cheerleaders in every endeavour— particularly to my mum and dad, Sean and Tamsin Hayes, for letting me write the majority of this book in their tiny cottage by the sea, which offers endless inspiration and much needed connection with nature. Finally, thank you to all those who discussed this book with me, made suggestions, and heard me out as I tried to paint a picture of happiness through these wonderful words—there are too many individuals to list but you will certainly know who you are if I bent your ear about it.